Create A Better YOU!
12 Essential Elements For Your Greatest Comeback EVER!

Copyright © 2013, 2016 Ryan C. Greene
www.ryancgreene.com

All Rights Reserved. No part of this publication may be reproduced, stored in a retrieval system, or transmitted in any form by means electronic, mechanical, photocopying, recording or otherwise, except for the inclusion of brief quotations in a review, without prior permission in writing from the publisher.

Cover design by: GreeneHouse Media, Print Division
Photography Courtesy of www.istockphoto.com

ISBN: 978-0-9842631-7-2

Printed in the USA

Published by
GreeneHouse Media
www.greenehousemedia.com

12 ESSENTIAL ELEMENTS FOR YOUR GREATEST COMEBACK EVER

CREATE A BETTER YOU!

RYAN C. GREENE

Dedication

*To Jordan and Jayden,
You are my inspiration to create a better me every day.
I adore you both and thank God every day for
blessing me to be the man you call Daddy.
I love you!*

TABLE OF CONTENTS

Introduction
9

Create A Better CONNECTION
11

Create A Better NOW
23

Create Better DREAMS
33

Create A Better ENVIRONMENT
43

Create Better HABITS
53

Create Better COMMUNICATION
63

Create Better RELATIONSHIPS
75

Create Better DECISIONS
85

Create Better FINANCES
95

Create A Better LEADER
105

Create Better VALUE
115

Create A Better STORY
123

Create A Better YOU!
135

About The Author
137

CREATE A BETTER YOU!

INTRODUCTION

"NET worth is judged by the assets you own. SELF worth is judged by the actions you take when you've lost it all." ~ James Worthy

What do you do when you're fed up with the cards you've been dealt in life? You either fold and surrender or you accept that maybe it's not the cards you've been dealt that's the problem, but rather how you've played those cards. You either go on blaming every other person, place or thing for your dissatisfaction or you look in the mirror and accept the fact that you're staring at your biggest problem.

I'm pretty certain if you asked around you'd find that you are not the only person who wants more out of their life. You're not the only person who's ever had dreams unfulfilled or obstacles not tackled. You'd probably find many people who are extremely successful only got there, either after they lost everything or after they came to the realization that "things" is not what makes them successful and fulfilled. So what is it then that differentiates those most successful people who achieve great things from those who just get stuck dreaming and wishing for a better life?

The answer lies within this book. The most successful and fulfilled people all realize that if they want a better life then they have to grow into a better person, worthy of and able to, handle that better life. The same now goes for you. If YOU want a better life, you must create a better YOU! "How do I create a better me?" you ask? That's what this book is going to teach you. They say experience is the best teacher so in this book I'm going to open myself up once again and share my personal experiences with you about my journey. Some of my greatest hardships have led to some of my most rewarding victories. Some of the most seemingly insignificant decisions along the way opened doors to my purpose and destiny. I'm going to tell my story and teach the lessons I learned from them in an effort to help you create the better life you desire and deserve.

Maybe you're like me and you're a "big idea" person. My mind is always churning with ideas and projects. Not just for me but for others too. People frequently reach out to me for advice on how to make their ideas better and grow their businesses. The hardest lesson I had to learn along the way was that I wasn't always ready to fulfill every idea that was dropped into my spirit. Just because I could come up with the plan on paper to make it work didn't mean I could execute them all right away. This frustration over the years manifested itself in many ways until eventually God clued me in to the secret: I had to GROW into that person who could handle those ideas.

So just like my previous books **_Success Is In Your Hand_** and **_My Little Black Book Of Leadership_**, this book was first written for ME. I had to live it first and test-drive the principles before I could share them with readers. If I'm going to spend time writing about the lessons and travel the country teaching them, then I had to know without a doubt that what I'm teaching works. That being said, these 12 essential elements for your greatest comeback ever that I'm teaching in this book WORK! There is no way you can focus on improving these 12 areas of yourself and not see a better life.

Maybe you already excel in some of them and that's great! Your current strengths and pure will and determination are probably what have gotten you to this point; but now it's time to put all the elements together and create the BEST you. Now it's time to fill in the missing elements and finally begin living your most fulfilled life! This book is your instruction manual for putting it all together. It's time to create a better life. It's time to create a better YOU!

Ryan C. Greene

CREATE A BETTER YOU!

Chapter One

Create A Better

CONNECTION

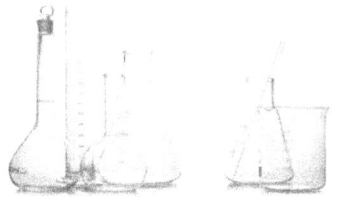

The last four years of my life have been pretty much a blur. I spent all of 2009-2012 basically living life as a zombie and going through the motions of a living person. I made sure to smile every day and always have a positive answer for the "How's it going?" that inevitably was asked by someone every day. I made sure to always dress like I was about my business even if building a business was the last thing on my mind. I made sure to always protect my kids from seeing the pain I was dealing with from not being around them every day. Shoot, I did such a great job of fooling everyone else that I was just fine, that I even fooled myself many times. I simply just kept moving in hopes that one day it was all be better.

I never planned to be divorced. Yet, there I was in January 2009 trying to pick up the pieces and figure out just what was I going to do with the rest of my life. Trying to look back and figure out how I had even gotten to that point where it all slipped away. What went wrong in those 10 years of marriage? How did we both get to the point where neither of us even wanted to fight to be together anymore? I can look back now and see clearly- we became disconnected. In many ways we were like two strangers sharing a house; mainly for the sake of the kids having both parents around.

Many factors contributed to this disconnect happening. It didn't simply happen overnight. Plenty of neglect, miscommunication, and distrust showed up; but personal growth, shifting values, and rearranged priorities played a role as well. The bottom line is the things that we felt connected us and drew us together 10 years earlier, simply weren't there any longer. We became disconnected. So one evening she told me she was leaving to stay with a friend and that was that. She never came back and our marriage was over.

So over the past four years I found myself on one end kicking feverishly to stay afloat and survive, while on the other end, just as quickly sinking to the bottom trenches of the ocean's abyss dying daily. Caught between questioning everything God ever promised me and wondering if I even wanted to be those things anymore. Debating if maybe a regular, mediocre insignificant life is really all I was supposed to live after all. Maybe I wasn't destined to make some great impact on the lives of others and I was to simply be relegated to a redundant life of a 9-5 job I hated.

I went from being on a known path going in a positive direction with tons of momentum in 2008 to slamming into a brick wall in 2009 and having it all come to a screeching halt. I no longer knew who I was. I no longer knew what I was meant to be in the world. I no longer knew what was most important for me? My life became one of desperation over destiny. I began subscribing to that mantra "I gotta do what I gotta do." Instead of doing what I was CALLED to do. I had lost all motivation to write and inspire others through talks, I stopped doing radio, I even stopped marketing myself as a speaker/author all

CREATE A BETTER YOU!

together! My main focus was on trying to survive "right NOW" and it didn't matter what else got sacrificed. I had literally lost everything so I was beyond trying to save the old me and was truly trying to discover who I was going to be next.

The problem was I was trying to do it all alone and with no real direction. I battled depression along the way mainly because I felt so alone and betrayed. No matter how hard I looked or how willing I was to "just get any job", that never seemed to come easy or bring me much joy. Add to that, no matter how many times I tried to figure things out on my own and do what others would call the safe bet, God wouldn't allow me to totally walk away from what He purposed me to be. No matter how much I tried to douse it, He never let that fire in me go totally out. It took me four years to get back to it but finally here I am releasing my fifth book with yet another testimony.

I found myself begging and praying to God to make things better, to give me a better life and one day I heard him tell me: "If you want a better life, you must create a better YOU!" Pretty much, God told me He has already prepared the way. The resources and blessings are simply waiting on ME to line up and grow to the level to handle and take advantage of them. I had a choice to either wallow in my sorrows and continue to blame my pain on everyone else or I could get up, take responsibility for the only person I could control, and become a better me.

As I surveyed my life and everything that had gotten me to that point and everything that was preventing me from getting to where God destined me to be, He showed me 12 essential elements that I needed to make better in myself in order to make my life better. These 12 elements are universal to anyone else who's in that same place I was in and is searching for a way out. You don't have to be called to be a professional speaker or a media personality like me. Your dreams and happiness may not be wrapped up in something as big as mine or others around you. But whatever your dreams are, wherever your happiness and fulfillment lies, you will never reach that place fully until you master becoming the best YOU first. The only way your life will get better is for YOU to get better.

The very first thing I had to accept was that I needed to **CREATE A BETTER CONNECTION**. When creating a better you, there are three levels of connection you must strengthen: spiritual, purpose and people.

STRENGTHEN YOUR SPIRITUAL CONNECTION

The first thing I had to accept on my journey to creating a better me was that I couldn't continue trying to do it alone. I couldn't neglect He who was directing the show. My darkest times when I felt most alone weren't because God had forsaken me, but because I had strayed away from Him. I couldn't expect to be my best me, my most powerful me, when I was disconnected from my power source. Before I worked on anything else I had to strengthen my spiritual connection.

The same goes for you. You may not be Christian like me, but hopefully you believe in some higher power for yourself. Prayerfully, you understand that no matter how much of a genius you feel you are on your own, "you didn't build this". Some people think faith is silly. They think having faith and trusting in God is a crutch for weak-minded people. I obviously don't see it that way. I think everything we see and experience was intelligently designed and created for a specific purpose. Every joy and pain we experience in life is for a greater reason that those who are most connected will learn and understand.

So how do you get more spiritually connected? What does spiritual connection to something you can't see, even look like? Well here's a few ways to get connected:

1) **Pray-** Prayer is nothing more than talking to God. Many people try to make this more complicated and elaborate than it needs

CREATE A BETTER YOU!

to be but praying is simply a conversation between you and God. It's where you share your thoughts, ideas, hopes, concerns, worries, desires etc with Him. Prayer is where you go to simply tell God what's on your mind.

2) **Listen-** Often times I hear people say "Maybe I'm not praying enough" or "God didn't answer my prayer". My first question to them is usually "Did you stick around long enough to listen for His answer? Too many times we get so caught up in telling God what we want and need from him that we aren't still long enough to hear his reply. We totally miss his answer or direction for us to go to receive that which we pray for. It's not enough to simply pray, but you must listen for the answers too.

3) **Read-** One of the great things about God is He gave us a manual to follow. It's up to each of us to read it and apply it to our lives but we must study the scriptures for the answers on how to better connect with God. There isn't an answer He doesn't provide on how to connect with Him and line up for His purpose for your life.

4) **Relationship-** Treat God just like you're dating Him. By that I simply mean if you were dating someone; you would call them daily, spend quality time with them, show them you love them in many ways, you would be on your best behavior around them and so on. So why not do the same with God? The more frequently you interact with Him, the more you make Him a part of everything you do, the closer and more connected you'll feel. You will begin to instinctively make decisions that would be more pleasing to Him simply because you're more focused on Him in all things you do.

5) **Give-** Before you close the book right here, I'm not collecting an offering! I'm talking about Praise & Worship. God requires and deserves our adoration and worship. The more we give that to Him the more submitted to His Will we become and the more he can use us to fulfill His purpose and plan for our lives. If God is going to give us the desires of our hearts, the least we can do is praise Him and be thankful for Him just being who He is.

A strong spiritual connection is Ground Zero. It's where it all begins and the foundation upon which you are going to create a better you. Once you've strengthened your spiritual connection, you can then move on to strengthening the next connection.

STRENGTHEN YOUR PURPOSE CONNECTION

Why are you here? What were you put on this earth to accomplish? What is your purpose? How deeply entrenched are you into achieving that purpose? What would your life be like if you walked away from purpose and did something else? Are you willing to live with those consequences?

These are some of the questions I asked myself weekly, if not daily, during that four year wilderness of mine. I knew what my purpose in life was but I also knew what my "right now" looked like and I couldn't for the life of me figure how to make the two of them work together. It was the pursuit of that very purpose that had gotten me into some of the mess I was in so how could I justify continuing that pursuit? I had lost everything, owed everybody, and was sapped dry of all creative inspiration. I wanted to do better and knew I was better than my circumstances but nothing seemed to be working. Still even after all of that, I knew there was no way I could live with myself if I walked away from my purpose.

CREATE A BETTER YOU!

I had to make a decision to reconnect and recommit to my purpose. I had to take an honest inventory of what I was doing and make some changes. I realized it wasn't my purpose that was to blame but my pursuit. I had to learn to live a dual life. I had to figure how to "Survive & Thrive". I had to find a way to survive right now and deal with my current circumstances while also remaining committed to my purpose and building toward my future so that I could thrive later. Once I was able to accept that responsibility, it began to free up my mind from the guilt and pain of the setbacks I had faced.

So what can you do to strengthen your purpose connection without jeopardizing your current life situation?

1) **Write out the purpose for your life and look at it every day-** Sometimes simply reading our purpose is all it takes to motivate us to keep pushing. I conduct a Dream Day Workshop with my good friends and fellow speakers, Michael Powell and Yolonda Coleman, and the keystone project of each Dream Day is to create a Dream Board. This board consists of pictures and words of all of your dreams and goals and serves as a visual reminder to help keep your purpose in front of you every day. Every morning before you begin your day and every night before you end it, your purpose should be on your mind.

2) **Develop your overall plan to fulfill your purpose-** Once you discover your purpose, you need to develop your plan to fulfill that purpose. Ask God to show you how He wants to use you to fulfill the plan for your life. Make the plan as detailed as possible. This is similar to a brainstorm session you may do at work but it's for your life. Just begin to list every idea that comes to mind and falls in line with your purpose. Don't worry about how outrageous the ideas may seem at this point. Some things may be for 15 years from now, but I wouldn't trust my memory to remember that idea in 15 years so write it down now.

12 ESSENTIAL ELEMENTS FOR YOUR GREATEST COMEBACK EVER!

3) **Choose the first project and start there-** Here's where a lot of people get tripped up. Once they've listed all these great ideas and can see how wonderfully they've laid out their life to be, they wanna jump and do it all at one time. Unfortunately, that method rarely ever works. The tried and true method of the most successful people is to choose one project and focus all of your energy and resources into making that one succeed. Once you've built that, you now have a track record of success upon which you can begin to expand and build more. So choose whichever idea is going to excite you the most, is the most tangible from your current position and will lead you to the next project. Focus and go to work on that!

4) **Work on that project every single day-** Remember, in the beginning you're in "Survive & Thrive" mode. So you're still busy with everything else in life. Your career, family and other obligations aren't going away but neither is your desire to create a better life. Knowing that you will only have limited time to pursue that purpose in the beginning, it's important that you set aside time every day to work towards that project you chose. Don't let anything else take away your allotted time for purpose development. As long as you remain committed to doing something every single day, by the end of one year you will see amazing results and be on your way to a better life!

5) **Engage with other purpose driven people-** It's important that you understand not everyone in your life is purpose driven. Many people you interact with on a daily basis probably don't even know what their purpose is, let alone pursue it. They simply live and they're good with that. So when you start walking in your purpose you're going to need to develop new associations. You will need to find people who

will keep you focused and push you harder towards your purpose. They may or may not be pushing toward similar goals as you but as long as they're pushing towards their purpose, many of their actions will be the positive reinforcement and affirmations you will need during your own pursuit. The "Law Of Associations" can't be ignored. If you're currently the average of your five closest friends and you're not living the best life you desire; then you will either need your four closest friends to begin their own pursuits along with you or you will have to find four new closest friends.

6) **Invest in your purpose-** No one is going to pour more time, money, and energy into your purpose than you will. When talking about reconnecting with your purpose, you have to be willing to make those investments. If your purpose came with a prospectus, what story would it tell? Where would it show your energy, time, and money have gone? Would it make others want to invest with you or run to someone else with a more solid track record? If simply having a purpose was all it took to succeed then I probably wouldn't have written this book and you probably wouldn't be reading it. But purpose alone isn't enough. You must be willing to make the necessary investment to see it come to fruition.

STRENGTHEN YOUR PEOPLE CONNECTION

You cannot do it alone! Let's just clear that up right now. You NEED people in your life to help you achieve anything noteworthy. John Maxwell said "No great accomplishment in the history of the world has ever been accomplished by just one person alone." If you believe "If it's gonna get done right then it's up to me to do it" then pardon me but GET OVER YOURSELF. If you're a leader and you feel it's still up to you to do whatever needs to be done right then that's more of a reflection on your poor leadership and people development than it is on the actual people you don't trust. If you want to create a better life for yourself then you are going to have to begin trusting others. You are going to have to begin leaning on and learning with other people in your life in order to accomplish greater things.

People are your most valuable resource. The more people with whom you have influence, the stronger your network and ability to get things done become. We've all heard the saying "It's not what you know, but who you know." Well if we've heard it all our lives, how bout we start believing it and acting accordingly?

My radio show **The Ryan & Bryan Show** was born out of a desire to strengthen my people connection. I had been doing my own radio show since 2006 but thanks to the advent of Facebook, I connected with my now co-host, Bryan Johnson. Bryan and I attended Hampton University together but didn't really know each other. Through our Facebook interaction we realized we had a lot in common and we unconsciously began building a huge following on our profile pages. Eventually, after much pushing from our friends, Bryan and I decided to seek a way to leverage our separate friend lists and bring all of our connections together. We built a Facebook Group where his friends and my friends could meet and interact and from that our live radio show was born.

Expanding my show to include Bryan was the best move I could have ever made. Our styles complement each other, listenership instantly doubled once his circle was introduced to the show, I'm enjoying radio again and now both of us are moving forward together in pursuit of our purpose. Now, what if I had said back in 2010 that I wasn't sharing my show with anyone? What if Bryan had let the fact that he never hosted radio stop him from joining the show? Who knows what would have happened but I'm just thankful we strengthened our people connection when we did. If you want a better life then you should do the same.

CREATE A BETTER YOU!
Journal

Chapter Notes:

_____

_____

_____

_____

_____

_____

_____

_____

I Need To Create Better Connections By:

_____

_____

_____

_____

_____

12 ESSENTIAL ELEMENTS FOR YOUR GREATEST COMEBACK EVER!

_____

_____

_____

Action Steps:

_____

_____

_____

_____

_____

_____

_____

_____

_____

CREATE A BETTER YOU!

Chapter Two

Create A Better

NOW

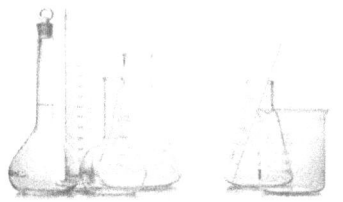

Eventually you reach a point where you simply have to START. You have to simply say regardless of what things look like around you right now, no matter what your present circumstances are, this is where your journey must BEGIN. You have to look at your life and decide to **CREATE A BETTER NOW.**

After I accepted the fact that my wife and I were not getting back together and I couldn't get work in Baltimore, I moved to Hampton, VA to work at my alma mater Hampton University. It was a tough decision to make such a drastic decision and pack up my life and move on just 2 weeks notice but I was going back to the one place where peace and joy had always been easy for me to find- my "Home By The Sea". So, in February 2010, the midst of the worst blizzard ever to hit Maryland, I packed up and moved to Hampton to start over.

12 ESSENTIAL ELEMENTS FOR YOUR GREATEST COMEBACK EVER!

My plan was to go to Hampton and reignite my fire, reconnect with who I used to be and refocus on my next phase of life. I wanted to gain some experience working at a university and then transfer back to Maryland in two years. Once I got there I was slapped with the reality that working for HU was a lot different from being a student at HU. That joy I was searching for never showed up. That motivation and direction I sought never found me. That fire never started burning inside me. I had so many plans on how things were supposed to go and one by one they all seemed to fail or be blocked by some other force. I found myself feeling more alone and empty than ever before.

I tend to be very future driven. Through my dark times it was my future that motivated me and kept me from giving up. My present, while hidden very well from most others, was a place of heartache, tears, doubt, and failures. There was nothing about where I was that brought me any joy or life on the inside. I was in a very unhappy, uninspiring place. I knew that wasn't who I was though. I knew I was better than that and capable of living a much more fulfilling powerful life and one day while sitting in my apartment it hit me.

I remembered a quote I heard years before "Where you are today is the results of decisions you made five years ago and where you'll be five years from now will be the result of decisions you make today." I don't even remember who said that but it was that quote that shook me back to life and made me realize that NOW was the most important key to creating the future I hoped for. I had to stop feeling sorry for myself and letting my current circumstances be my excuses as to why I couldn't operate in my gifts right now.

It was then when I accepted the fact that I AM an author right NOW! I AM a professional speaker right NOW! I AM a media personality right NOW! Right NOW! Even in the midst of all my mess I had to confess that I was my future right NOW. I had to begin doing the activities of a speaker, an author and a media personality all over again right then.

CREATE A BETTER YOU!

My main focus had to be on doing my best to be who I was created to be right in the moment and midst of all the confusion.

So what did I do? I began to find every opportunity to put myself back in the game and did it! Slowly but surely I was getting back to at least doing the things I knew I was supposed to be doing. I began marketing my books again. I began blogging in an effort to re-establish my online presence as a writer. I began to offer my services as a book designer so that even if I wasn't writing my own books, I was still getting back into the publishing industry in some fashion. I began to take smaller speaking gigs just to get back into "speaking shape". I was beginning to feel those juices flowing again. I was on my way back!

It wasn't about how much money I was making at the time, but how much activity I had going. I had to create a better Now by doing the thing before I expected to get paid from the thing. I was beginning to feel alive again and that feeling was more valuable than anything else. I was finding a way to work on being what I said I was every single day. Even when my circumstances around me were the same, my mindset and disposition were improving. I was still living in Hampton, still away from my kids, still overcoming the setbacks I was facing, but I was pressing toward the mark in spite of.

Today's Now looks much better than my Now of back then all because I chose to make it better. Every day I strive to make this the best NOW I can. I'm still steadfastly focused on the future, however I'm committed to also making sure right now it the best I can make it. It doesn't always mean it looks good on paper but as long as I can say I put my best forward each day then that was the best Now I could make it.

What does your Now look like? Is it conducive to you having a better life? What will your life look like 5 years from today if your now doesn't change? Are you happy with those possibilities? If not then it's time to create a better **NOW.**

12 ESSENTIAL ELEMENTS FOR YOUR GREATEST COMEBACK EVER!
LET TODAY BE THE LAST DAY YOUR CIRCUMSTANCES BE YOUR COP-OUT

So you're looking at your present life and you're not happy. In your mind life sucks right now and it's all because of your current situation and circumstances. You feel like you can never move forward because of how bad things are right now for you. Guess what my response is to that? "SO WHAT?!" Starting today "So what?!" needs to also be your response to your current circumstances.

For years you have allowed your past to have rule over your present while simultaneously sabotaging your future and enough is enough. Let today be the last day you allow your circumstances to be your cop-out. Your past failures and missteps can no longer be the reason why you can't achieve your goals, but let them be your motivation for why you MUST achieve your goals. Every successful person has some situation or mistake they made that they could have allowed to hold them back. The difference is those people decided to use their stumbling blocks as stepping stones into their greatness.

Maybe you have a criminal record. Maybe you have a poor relationships track record. Maybe you have been a piss poor parent. No matter what your challenge has been, no matter how much society tells you that you cannot succeed because of it, make today the day you decide to no longer be bound captive by the dark cloud of your mistakes and short comings. Decide today that YOUR story will be the story of the one who overcame in spite of.

It's easy to look at your current situation and accept that you cannot live any better than you are because of the cards stacked against you. But truly great people, abundantly successful people, don't take the easy road. Stop accepting your self-imposed excuses that allow you to live a mediocre life and begin today to press for a higher mark right from where you stand. Decide today that you will never use your current situation as a cop-out again.

CREATE A BETTER YOU!
USE WHAT YOU HAVE TODAY AS YOUR SPRINGBOARD TO BETTER

It doesn't take much to make yourself better. It takes things like hard work, determination and desire but it doesn't take a bunch of *stuff*. If we're talking about creating a better NOW then you need to take an inventory of what you have right now and how can you parlay that into small immediate successes that will springboard you to bigger successes. What skills do you have right now? Who do you know right now? What information do you have access to right now that can help you improve your current situation?

When I was faced with figuring out how to create a better NOW for myself, the first resource I knew I had to tap into was my voice. Not my literal voice (although I've been told that's nice too) but my voice of influence. I had experience in radio, had authored several books and was a fledgling public speaker so I knew people were willing to pay attention to my words as long as I was saying something worth paying attention to. It didn't cost money to write a blog and it was free to host a radio show online. So just like that, using what I had at the time, I jumped back in the game.

So what do you have today? What is going to be your springboard to a better NOW and a better life? Find every little thing you can use right now to begin the process of creating a better NOW for you. Five years from now you will look back on this moment and be amazed at just how different your life looks all from the small beginnings you made right now.

Start writing that book or blog post today. Apologize to your spouse for your mistakes today. Apply for that new job you've been dreaming of today. Shoot that video of you giving advice in your area of expertise and post it on YouTube today. Start that Facebook Fan Page and begin promoting your business today. Setup an account on BlogTalkRadio.com and start hosting your own show today. Begin reading The Bible daily and fasting to draw closer to God today. I could keep going but the point is to figure it out and start it TODAY. If you think lack of money is the reason your dreams aren't coming true then you haven't developed your dreams enough. You have the resources around you right now to make things better today. You just have to do it!

STOP BEING HELD HOSTAGE BY YOUR PAST

Jim Rohn said one of the biggest factors in determining our Positive Mental Attitude is how we feel about our past. Our feelings about our past can grip us in such a way that we are no good in our present or our future. Some people are held hostage by their own past decisions and others may be held hostage by the effects of actions of others from our past. Either way, in order to create a better NOW or a better you, letting go of the bondage of the past is critical.

Guilt from your past mistakes is real. Some mistakes we make absolutely should make us feel guilty about them. But in order to move on past them, you must accept the guilt, pay the consequences, forgive yourself, and then give yourself permission to move on with your life. I'm no psychologist or counselor so I'm just telling you *what* needs to be done, but I'd advise you to seek professional help for more advice on *how* to do it if the guilt has gripped you too tightly.

Anger is another emotion that grips many people who have been hurt in the past by others. Successful people don't generally walk around angry at the world. There are constructive ways to use your anger as fuel, but just being angry all the time isn't healthy at all. If someone has hurt you in the past, forgiveness is going to be your first step to healing. You may never know all the answers to why they hurt you, but the sooner you can forgive and truly free up that space in your mind and heart you allow them to occupy, the sooner you will be

CREATE A BETTER YOU!

healed and able to move on for yourself. People spend more time angry at folks who either: a) aren't even thinking about them b) have moved on already or c) don't even know they hurt you to begin with.

The longer you allow your current frame of mind to be manipulated by your past, the longer you will struggle to ever see better days. Letting go is not easy but it is necessary. Free your heart and your mind from the pain and stigma of your past and allow that space to be rented by better tenants such as JOY, PEACE, and HAPPINESS.

12 ESSENTIAL ELEMENTS FOR YOUR GREATEST COMEBACK EVER!

Journal

Chapter Notes:

_____

_____

_____

_____

_____

_____

_____

_____

I Need To Create A Better Now By:

_____

_____

_____

_____

_____

CREATE A BETTER YOU!

_____

_____

_____

Action Steps:

_____

_____

_____

_____

_____

_____

_____

_____

_____

_____

12 ESSENTIAL ELEMENTS FOR YOUR GREATEST COMEBACK EVER!

CREATE A BETTER YOU!

Chapter Three

Create Better

DREAMS

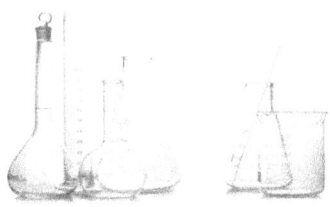

What are your dreams? What desires and goals are you chasing? How close are you to achieving them? How in line are your dreams with God's purpose for your life? Are your dreams BIG ENOUGH? Do people call you crazy for the dreams you've shared with them? Do your own dreams scare even you sometimes at how outrageous they sound? No? Then guess what? You're not dreaming big enough! You need to **CREATE BETTER DREAMS.**

Most people's dreams start from a place of desire in their heart. There's something out there they want so they imagine in their mind what it would be like to have it. Then something called reality begins to kick in and kills all the dreams. Sometimes reality is ushered in by outside forces and people while other times it's ourselves who allow our future possibilities to be killed by our current realities. Wherever it's coming from, it's up to you to stop allowing it to kill your dreams.

12 ESSENTIAL ELEMENTS FOR YOUR GREATEST COMEBACK EVER!

I'm no stranger to big dreams. That being said, I'm also no stranger to big doubters of my dreams. Some of my dreams were so big and seemed so outrageous that eventually I stopped sharing them with certain people who simply couldn't grasp them. I stopped trying to explain how something that had never been done before in my family was not only going to be done but going to be done by ME. I knew that if it had been accomplished before by someone else then it was possible that it could also be accomplished by me as well. Then reality began to set in.

Yup, even I fell victim to reality and all the doubt from outside and within. What was in front of me was a track record of well intentioned plans that had failed to be fulfilled for one reason or another. Some lacked the resources (i.e. time, money or people), some were victims of poor timing and some failed due to poor execution. Yet here I was trying to do it all over yet again. I was either a glutton for punishment, certifiably crazy or truly wired to do this. No matter how many times I wanted to quit speaking and writing, I kept getting pulled back into this arena.

This time it was different though. I didn't realize it at the time but there was something noticeably different about my dreams I was laying out back in 2010. My dreams weren't as big. I wasn't aiming as high. They all had contingency plans. My dreams seemed to be more focused on what I needed right then as opposed to what I needed for my future. I found myself dreaming out of desperation and not for my destiny. Somehow I convinced myself that the same activities that were fueling my dreams the past 4 years were now only worth a quarter of the return. It was like I was selling myself short and my dreams had become the "Plan B" instead of the main thing.

I had lost faith in my dreams and the ability to achieve them. I started adopting sayings like "make ends meet" and "backup plans" and "just in case this doesn't work" while setting the plans for my future. The financial goals I once felt were very attainable were now being met with self-doubt and defeatist language like "Those numbers are too high." and "No way am I gonna make that much." I was already defeating myself and my dreams before I had given them a real shot at manifesting. Instead of setting goals to change my family's destiny forever, I was setting goals that would make me enough to survive on for the year. The sad part was I didn't even realize I was doing it.

The biggest problem with setting my goals too low was that while on one side the numbers may have appeared more attainable, the flip side was that the goals offered such diminishing returns that it made it nearly impossible to be motivated to even go after them. The small returns I was chasing made the effort not even worth it. Then I woke up and realized I still had to put the exact same work into writing a book whether it sold 300 copies or 30,000 copies. The same time went into developing a one day seminar whether 15 people registered or 150 did. So if the work on the front end was the same, why would I sell myself short by not even trying to reach the maximum goal on the backend?

That's when I made the decision to create bigger dreams. I had to go all in with my dreams and get back to who I was. Instead of making my dreams smaller, I made them bigger but I also made them SMARTER. I was now in a position of being wiser because of my mistakes and miscues so I knew the problem was not the size of the dream but the actions of the dreamer. I began to create bigger dreams and was once again motivated to go after them. Only this time I had a better more focused plan. This time I had experience on my side to make my dreams work.

So I began to list all the dreams I had for my life and how they aligned with God's purpose for my life and went to work. I learned my lesson. This time instead of trying to do everything at one time like before, I chose one part of the dream and focused my efforts there and began putting together the plan to make it happen. This book was the first piece of the new bigger dream. I decided I had to first share my story with others and help them get over the hurdles of their lives in order to create better lives for themselves. But I had written books before so where was the "bigger"?

The "bigger" came when the idea that this would be my calling card for the next year was dropped in my spirit. Never had I designed an entire year of programming around one book or theme like I did with this one. My bigger mission became to help everyone who was ready to "Create A Better YOU!" So now after reading this book the message doesn't end there. You can visit www.RyanCGreene.com and register for monthly webinars, live workshops and retreats all geared around creating a better YOU! You can even watch my online television show "Create A Better YOU! w/ Ryan C. Greene" and constantly work on creating a better life for yourself. So that's what I did. What are you going to do to **CREATE BETTER DREAMS**?

DREAMS ARE MAN-MADE, PURPOSE IS GOD-MADE, DESTINY IS WHERE THE TWO OF THEM MEET

God has designed each of us for a specific purpose. He has put in us everything we need to fulfill the purpose He has for our lives. Whatever it is He has called you to achieve in life, He has already paved the way for you to walk in that purpose. The problem most people face however is finding out just what that purpose is. For some like myself, God's purpose for my life was made pretty clear to me. For others, they struggle with discerning between their passions and God's purpose for their life.

Then there are your dreams. Your dreams are man-made. They come from your own passions, desires and talents. Your dreams consist of the goals and accomplishments you wish to achieve throughout your lifetime. You are free to develop your own dreams. Your dreams hopefully line up with your skill set or else they may be unrealistic dreams. If you are in tune with your purpose, your dreams most likely line up with that purpose and run in tandem. God knows what He's purposed for your life but He's not gonna purpose you to do or be something that doesn't excite you. You won't dread living in God's purpose for your life.

Then there is destiny. That place where your dreams meet with God's purpose for your life is that place called "DESTINY". When your dreams are coming true and they line up with God's purpose for your life, that is the magnum opus, the epitome of success, the high life. When you can wake up every day doing what you love to do and know it's also what you were created to do, that's when you know you are living your best life.

SHIFT FROM DREAMS OF DESPERATION TO DREAMS OF DESTINY

Now that you know what destiny is, why would you want to experience anything less than that level of living? For most people, myself included, who are struggling to break through to a new level of success, one big factor holding them back is the level of their dream. When you dream from a survival mindset you can only dream of getting by. You can only dream as big as making ends meet and saving the little you already have. Those are Dreams of Desperation.

Dreams of Destiny allow you to dream bigger than your current situation and see yourself the way God sees you. Dreaming from a Destiny Mindset allows you to open your mind to dream as if you already are the person you were purposed to be and you are simply waiting for the manifestation of those dreams. You are simply waiting for and working toward the outward confirmations of the inward declarations.

Believe me I understand what it feels like to have nothing and all you can think about is surviving through the month. That's a terribly dark place to be, let alone trying to dream about anything more than which bill collectors aren't going to extend you anymore grace periods. A life of lack is depressing. It makes you feel less than human and even dirty at times. What I've found however; is when you're broke, no matter if you dream big or small at the moment, you're still broke. So why not dream big, see your life from a destiny perspective and launch from there?

That doesn't mean you live in some fantasy world and ignore all that's going on around you. What it does mean however is you release the hold all of those material things have on you by accepting that if you lose them now, it's not the end of the world and that simply makes room for new things and opportunities. If you found a way to acquire them once, you can find a way to acquire them again. Your current season of lack is just a proving ground for your time of destiny and abundance. How you operate now with little shows God how you will act with much. Never give up on your destiny simply because you are currently struggling.

DON'T LET THE BELIEF LEVEL OF OTHERS LIMIT YOUR DREAM LEVEL

If you have friends who are constantly dissuading you from going after your dreams then it's time for you to find some new friends. We all have fallen victim to sharing a dream that excited us with a friend or relative only to have them shoot it down for some reason. Sometimes those friends may have valuable insight and justification for shooting it down but most times, if those friends aren't experts in the area of that dream, all they're really doing when shooting down your dream is telling you that your dream is too big for THEM.

Pledge today to never again forfeit your dreams because it is too big for people in your circle. Rather than forfeit your big dreams, forfeit those small thinking friends for the time being and go after your

CREATE A BETTER YOU!

dreams! Once you achieve your dreams they'll either come back around or you'll meet better bigger thinking new friends along the way. It is not your responsibility to make sure your friends are comfortable with your dreams. It IS your responsibility however to make sure you passionately and vigorously pursue your dreams. It IS your responsibility to provide the best lifestyle possible for your family.

Your friends don't mean any harm. They really think they are helping you by warning you of the dangers of chasing your big dreams. The reality though is they are projecting their fears and uncertainties onto your ideas and you have to be wise enough to recognize when that happens and strong enough to stand up against it when it does. The bottom line is we don't pick our friends first based on their expertise in the areas important to our lives. We pick them on compatibility. Since we don't pick them based on any level of expertise, then why do we so often let our non-expert friends dictate to us what plans for our lives are best?

If you want a better life, you have to be able to see that life before you live it. You have to dream it before you can make the dream come true. So stop dreaming small dreams and begin dreaming your biggest dreams again! Open your mind up to the possibilities in front of you and allow your mind to really accept that those dreams can come true and they can come true for YOU!

12 ESSENTIAL ELEMENTS FOR YOUR GREATEST COMEBACK EVER!

Journal

Chapter Notes:

_____
_____
_____
_____
_____
_____
_____
_____
_____

I Need To Create Better Dreams By:

_____
_____
_____
_____
_____
_____

CREATE A BETTER YOU!

_____

_____

_____

Action Steps:

_____

_____

_____

_____

_____

_____

_____

_____

_____

12 ESSENTIAL ELEMENTS FOR YOUR GREATEST COMEBACK EVER!

CREATE A BETTER YOU!

Chapter Four

Create A Better

ENVIRONMENT

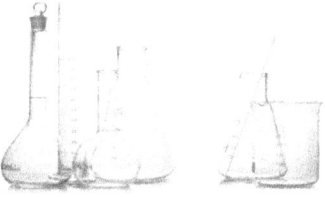

In the Fall of 1992 I had a big decision to make. What college was I going to attend the next Fall? Being from Baltimore and going to a predominantly African American high school, the obvious first local choice was Morgan State University. Morgan was about 20 minutes from my home and as an H.B.C.U. (Historically Black College & University) just about all my classmates who were going to college locally were going to Morgan. It would have been an easy transition but going to Morgan State at that time also came with a stigma of going to the "13th Grade" as we called it back then. Morgan has come a long way since my high school graduation but back then it wasn't such a badge of honor to say you were going to Morgan State.

Then there was Towson University. Towson was the alternative for those who wanted to stay local but not go to a "black" school. Towson had a better reputation and better just about everything else when compared to Morgan. It was at Towson where I got my first taste of Greek Life during a weekend visit and knew I was going to pledge Alpha Phi Alpha Fraternity, Inc., whenever I got to college. Towson had a bowling alley! But what Towson didn't have was my desired major!

Enter Howard University. I honestly don't even remember how I first heard of Howard University but I'm thinking it had something to do with the girl I had the biggest crush on in high school who graduated the year before going to Howard? Whatever the reason, I instantly fell in love with the school without even seeing it. It was a bigger and better H.B.C.U. than Morgan State and it was in Washington D.C. so it was 45 minutes away from home. Not too close but not too far away either. It was called "The Mecca" and this was around the time going to an H.B.C.U. was the thing to do so I was all ready to go to Howard!

Then my girlfriend at the time started talking about some small school in Virginia called Hampton University. She was already accepted and attending there in the Fall. I had heard of Hampton, Virginia because my mother used to go to the jazz festival every year but I never knew about the school. Hampton was kind of the best of all worlds. It was part of what's unofficially known as the "Black Ivy League" of H.B.C.U.'s which meant it had a stellar reputation. It was half the size of Howard so it was more intimate. It was 4 hours away from home which meant freedom. And it had the prettiest campus and women!

So how did I make my decision on which school to ultimately attend? I had to evaluate each school and decide which environment fit most with my goals and lifestyle and which gave me the best opportunity to grow and succeed. If I chose Morgan or Towson, I'd be at home and the temptation to get a job while in school would hinder my finishing school on time. At that time Baltimore was also the Teen Pregnancy Capital of the U.S. so I felt I ran the very real risk of getting

CREATE A BETTER YOU!

a girl pregnant if I stayed at home and that was NOT an option. Come to find out Morgan lost my application and Towson didn't have my major so those decisions were pretty much made for me.

So it was between Howard and Hampton even though in my mind I had already chosen Howard. That is until I visited the campus. I was born and raised in the suburbs. "The County" is what we locals call it. Contrary to most people's beliefs, all of Baltimore is not like what you saw on "The Wire". We don't all talk like Snoop, we don't all deal drugs and we don't all live in the 'hood. So when I got to Howard's campus and realized it was an "open campus" (meaning anyone could walk on campus at anytime) in the heart of the city; that was a culture shock to me. Compare that to the "closed campus" of Hampton University on the waterfront of Hampton, VA with plush manicured lawns and no outsiders it was a no-brainer for me.

I never even applied to Howard. I traded in all of my Howard Gear for Hampton Gear and chose the environment that felt most like home to me- Hampton University. It was scary at first when I watched my mom drive off as she left me on the steps of my dorm, but over the next four years Hampton proved time and time again to be the absolute right choice for me. I entered as a cornball from Baltimore but eventually I made lifelong friends, created a singing group and began songwriting my Freshman Year, got involved in many organizations and pledged Alpha Phi Alpha my Sophomore Year, developed my leadership skills as President of The Student Union Board my Junior Year and started HU's Spring Fest which still goes on to this day. By Senior Year I was elected Senior Class President.

Graduating from high school I had a goal to create a better me and I knew even then how important creating a better environment was in that process. The environment I chose gave me the atmosphere to succeed and right now you need to figure how you can create a better environment around you. If you want things to get better for you then you need to **CREATE A BETTER ENVIRONMENT.**

12 ESSENTIAL ELEMENTS FOR YOUR GREATEST COMEBACK EVER!
IF YOU'RE NOT TRYING TO BE THERE, DON'T BE THERE

What sense would it make for a recovering alcoholic to hang out at bars? Why would a married man hang out in strip clubs? Why would someone addicted to gambling hang out at a Las Vegas casino? Why would someone who's trying to live right hang with people who are living foul? Where are you spending your time? Is it conducive with the life you claim you want to live? If you're not trying to be about that life then why would you hang in the spots frequented by those who are about whatever that life is?

Listen (well read) closely- YOU ARE NOT THAT STRONG! I know that may have been a punch to the gut but believe me, you are not the first person who tricked themselves into believing you can surround yourself in certain less that productive environments and it not faze you. It absolutely fazes you. Whether you want to accept it early on before you see it or wait until later when the results negatively impact your life, where you go affects how you grow.

Putting yourself in negative environments doesn't automatically mean you are going to pick up the bad behaviors of the environment but it will definitely stunt your growth. Growth comes not just from learning but from sharing. When you are in an environment where you are not able to share with like-minded people, your own growth is stunted. It's like casting your pearls among the swine. Why would you do that? Unless you feel like God called you specifically to go into an environment and call people out, you would be best served to stay out yourself.

The wrong environment is also more than a physical place. You could find yourself in the wrong environment mentally, emotionally or spiritually. If you are in a committed relationship with someone and you are having inappropriate communications with someone else, you are in a negative environment. Get out of there! If you call yourself a Christian yet no one can tell from your behaviors, you are in a negative environment. Get out of there! If your mind is full of negative thoughts and depression controls you when you want to be happy, you are in a negative environment. Get out of there! If you say you don't want to be what the environment produces, then don't be in the environment.

PUT YOURSELF IN PLACES AND POSITIONS TO SUCCEED

Once you have removed yourself from the negative environments, then what? Now you must surround yourself in positive environments that help push you closer to creating a better life. Find out where people who do what you want to do hang out and go there. Find out what people like the person you want to become read and begin reading those things. You can't wait until you actually become the better you to finally start changing your surroundings. You have to start right now.

Join a church. Volunteer for a non-profit organization. Coach a youth league sport. Start a Girl Scout Troop. Join a Network Marketing Company. Find anything positive that will allow you to flourish and engage in positive activities while meeting new people along the way. You never know where that next connection will come from that will launch you into the next phase of your life. Putting yourself in places and positions to succeed at least gets you on the playing field. As the opportunities come, it's up to you to hit the ball out of the park.

You may be surprised at just how big an impact an environment change can have on your disposition. Sometimes people don't know any better because they simply haven't seen or experienced any better. Moving on is difficult to do when you have roots somewhere but for many people, getting out of the old neighborhood is just what the doctor ordered. I love my hometown of Baltimore but Lord knows more Baltimoreans need to travel a bit and see how life is done in other places and incorporate some of those mindsets into the city. Just about every majorly successful person from Baltimore had to leave the city before they finally got their breakthrough. It may be time for you to expand your horizons and stop being afraid to change zip codes.

CHANGE WHAT YOUR MENTAL ENVIRONMENT LOOKS LIKE

In every book I've written I discuss "The Personal Development Puzzle". This Puzzle gives the keys to putting together the pieces of growing your mindset and improving your value in the marketplace. You must grow your mindset before you can grow your paycheck. Personal development is that important that I find a way to include this piece in every book. And if you want to create a better life then you are going to have to change your mental environment.

A USA Today poll showed that 25% of Americans polled have not read a single book in the last year. I have heard numbers even higher than that. Regardless of your age, all that you know today is not enough to get you through the rest of your life. Even if your mission in life is to simply skate through and do nothing with your life, every day you must learn new ways to survive by being the best worthless bump on a log you can be. When it comes to personal development I live by the mantra "You must become the person you want to be BEFORE your business card says you are."

If you aspire to be great then you must follow the best practices of great people. You must read the books they read, go to the trainings they go to, do the things they do. You have to become that person in your mind and in your practices before you actually become that person in your position. What good would come out of you being elevated to a position that you were not mentally equipped to fulfill?

CREATE A BETTER YOU!

God will not put more on you than you can bear so if you are not mentally ready to bear the responsibilities that go with higher levels of success then you will not be elevated to those levels.

Life is not fair, life is JUST. Life gives you what you DESERVE and not what you want. You may *want* to be the Sales Manager at your job but if you do not study your craft, learn to work with others, develop your leadership skills, put in the extra work and grow into that position; then you *deserve* to be just an account executive. You may *want* to earn $250K a year but as long as you demand your company gives you a set salary as opposed to you earning unlimited bonuses, complain about how much life sucks, focus on the problems and not the solutions and get paid for what you do instead of what you know; then you *deserve* to only earn $40K a year. If you want more you have to grow more.

For an in depth look at how you can begin making personal development a natural part of your everyday life I would encourage you to purchase my first book **_Success Is In Your Hand_** and work through the exercises. For now I will share some of the bullet points on the Four Keys to the personal development puzzle.

Key #1: Watch what goes into you. The basic tenet of personal development is taking care that you fill your mind with positive inputs. In order to get good things out of you, you must first put good things into you. Reading self-help books like this one shows you are serious about filling your mind with positive life changing messages.

Key #2: Watch what comes out of you. When you begin to change what goes into you it inevitably changes what comes out of you. Everything from your attitude, your vision, your appearance, to the way you treat other people will begin to improve. People will begin seeing a difference in you probably before you even see the difference. You will begin to attract other like-minded people who will play major roles in your success.

12 ESSENTIAL ELEMENTS FOR YOUR GREATEST COMEBACK EVER!

Key #3: The Law of Associations. As you begin to grow on the inside, your senses will be more alert to the destructive behaviors and people with whom you were once connected. Your current friends will either have to change their mindsets and grow with you or you will ultimately out grow them. A tell-tale sign that you are on the right path with your growth will be when your friends get angry with you and tell you that "you changed."

Key #4: Appreciate who you become along the way. Personal development is a lifelong journey. There is no finish line or final destination where you can say "I've arrived." The joy is in the journey and knowing that you have become a better person along the way. Unlocking your full potential and walking in your designed purpose is the ultimate reward for a life dedicated to personal development.

CREATE A BETTER YOU!
Journal

Chapter Notes:

_____
_____
_____
_____
_____
_____
_____
_____

I Need To Create A Better Environment By:

_____
_____
_____
_____
_____

12 ESSENTIAL ELEMENTS FOR YOUR GREATEST COMEBACK EVER!

_____

_____

_____

Action Steps:

_____

_____

_____

_____

_____

_____

_____

_____

CREATE A BETTER YOU!

Chapter Five

Create Better

HABITS

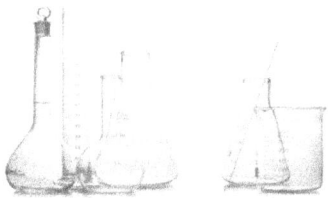

If you want to be successful you have to do what successful people do. If you want a better life, do what people with lives better than yours do. Adopt their habits and you will adopt their lifestyle. Adjust your behaviors so that they begin to line up with the behaviors of someone living the kind of life you desire to live. Habits are things you do over and over until the behavior becomes subconscious and part of who you are. It's the actions that make you who you are whether you do them on purpose or without even thinking about them. Show me your habits and I'll show you your future.

In April 2001 I entered the Network Marketing industry. I did like most people who have ever joined or been asked to look at a home-based opportunity do and I went to a hotel meeting for a presentation. The room was full of excited Independent Associates all holding on to the dream of financial independence and helping others along the way. I was 26 years old with an entrepreneur's heart so once I saw the services, heard a few success stories and saw the money that was on the table to be made I was in! I joined Pre-Paid Legal Services, Inc., (now Legal Shield, Inc.) on the spot and hit the ground running.

Here's what I loved about the company's leadership- the first thing I was told to do was attend a Corporate TRAINING. Right off the bat it was instilled in associates that in order to be successful in the company, and even the industry, you had to learn the habits of those who were already successful. I went to my first training and it was conducted by a former postal worker and a former retail manager who were both at the time making six-figures a year with the company. Surely I could have walked in thinking "Hey I have a college degree and x-number years of sales experience. What can you teach me about being a successful sales person?". Instead I walked in with the mindset of "I don't care what your background is, you're making way more money than I am so I want to learn everything you know about how to succeed in this industry."

I chose to humble myself and be a sponge to those gentlemen. I soaked up every nugget they gave me on how to build a successful network marketing team and within 2 years I had reached the top position in the company of Bronze Executive Director. But here's the thing- the biggest lesson they taught me about how to build a successful organization was not how to give a presentation, it was not how to prospect new reps, it wasn't even how to explain the compensation plan. The biggest lesson they taught me was how to become a better me. They taught me that the first thing any prospect is going to buy is ME so I should spend 80% of my time sharpening my axe (building myself) and 20% chopping the tree (selling my product).

At that point, while it was still a great financial opportunity, Network Marketing was no longer just about how much money I could make. It became more about how much I could grow. How personally developed could I become? It was more about me seeing how much I

CREATE A BETTER YOU!

could master the habits of those successful mentors I now had and how I could I transfer those skills into every other facet of my life. By creating better habits for myself I would not only succeed in that Network Marketing Company but in any other venture I decided to embark upon.

For me, the first thing I did was change what I watched on TV. No more News! News has to be the most depressing hour of the day and if that's not enough, it's on 24 hours a day! Who needs that in their lives when they're trying to create a better life? Then it was no more bubblegum for the brain programs like Reality TV, Competition Shows and Celebrity Gossip Shows. Eventually I stopped watching TV all together with the exception of a few shows and live sporting events. The amazing thing was I never missed watching TV! Not watching TV became a habit and now quite frequently I'll be in a room with a television and it never crosses my mind to turn it on. I never realized how much time I wasted sitting in front the boob tube watching other people fulfill their dreams instead of chasing after my own.

The next habit I began was reading. I never knew how much great information was hidden in these things called books. I had never read for fun before joining Legal Shield but now I don't even feel right if I'm not reading something to help me grow. The knowledge I gained from simply committing to read every day set me so far apart from my peers who were not committing to that same habit. I gained a world of new mentors whom I'd never met, all through reading their books. I learned that becoming a lifelong learner was one of the best habits to creating a better life. Now look at me. I'm the one writing the books! Maybe I'll be the inspiration to get you to write your book now.

Finally, I had to get into the habit of positive thinking. I know that may seem like an unusual thing to list in the "habits" category but early on I most definitely had to learn to think positively. I had to be deliberate in making sure the thoughts I let manifest in my mind were positive in nature and purpose. Surely we all could run down a litany of things to complain about in our lives and people who make our lives all the more difficult to live but what I learned from my success coaches was that time I wasted on complaining was better served on positive thoughts and ideas. I gravitated towards daily affirmations as my means of maintaining a positive mindset. I took time every day to list affirmations and future truths about my life as if they were already happening and just that simple habit would keep my mind focused on the right things even during the tough times.

We're talking about creating a better rest of your life. The question isn't should you create better habits, it's why wouldn't you?! Why wouldn't you make the effort to totally change your behaviors if it means it will lead to the better life you desire? Here's a daily affirmation you can start with: "I am creating a better life by **CREATING BETTER HABITS**".

WHAT YOU DO, YOU BECOME

Time for a little quiz.

Q. What do you call someone who paints?
A. A painter.

Q. What do you call someone who sings?
A. A singer.

Q. What do you call someone who smokes?
A. A smoker.

Do you see the theme here? What you DO, you BECOME. That's true in all areas of life. So what are you doing? Show me what you are doing and I will show you what you are becoming. Now ask yourself the question, "Is what I'm becoming, what I really want to be?" If your answer is "no" then you better change what you do. I've always heard that if you continually do anything for 21 consecutive days then by Day 22 it should be a habit and part of what you do automatically. The reality is that most people never make it through the first 21 days when trying to change their behaviors. The average New Year's Resolution is broken within the first 7 days of the New Year. That's pretty sad.

People tend to realize when their behaviors are counter-productive to a successful life but changing those behaviors is difficult once they're engrained into your being. Those negative behaviors have become habits. They have become what you do and therefore have become who you are. The positive spin to that is you can get positive behaviors just as engrained into your being as the negatives but usually it takes a lot more work to do the right thing as opposed to doing what feels good right now.

If you want to create better habits in your life then it's time to take inventory on all of your behaviors and begin coming up with a game plan to tackle them one by one. Trying to quit smoking is going to take a different type of game plan than trying to read a chapter a day of a self-help book. Know who you want to become and begin doing those things and creating those habits to become that person.

WHAT IS YOUR DAILY SUCCESS SCHEDULE?

Success doesn't happen by mistake. Successful people are successful on purpose. They don't simply wake up each morning and things just go their way. Successful people have a plan and they work their plan. They understand that time is one of their most valuable resources and they choose not to waste it. What is your Daily Success Schedule? What is it that you do every morning, afternoon and evening to ensure that your actions are moving you in the right direction to living a better life? Don't have one? If not, let's change that!

When I started my personal development quest and began improving my habits I didn't have a Daily Success Schedule either. I heard Brian Tracy speak on how to overcome procrastination in his book **_Eat That Frog_**. I had read Stephen Covey's **_7 Habits Of Highly Effective People_** and purchased my Franklin Planner. I almost had John C. Maxwell's **_21 Irrefutable Laws Of Leadership_** memorized, yet I still had not made myself a daily schedule to adhere too. I was still settling for shooting off from the hip every day expecting things to simply fall into place. Guess what? It didn't work. The experts were right and I had to change.

Here's an example of what a Daily Success Schedule looks like:

6:00 AM: Prayer and meditation
6:30 AM: Read for 30 minutes
7:00 AM: Workout
8:00 AM: Get dressed for work
12:00 PM: Work on "Plan B" during lunch
5:00 PM: Listen to audio book on ride home from work
6:00 PM: Family time and dinner
8:00 PM: Work on "Plan B" some more

This is a pretty generic template that can be customized based on your lifestyle and goals. Your "Plan B" may be a home based business in which you make prospecting calls during that time. It may be time for you to work on writing your book. It can be whatever is YOURS. Wherever you passion lies, you should make room to express that in some form or fashion each day. Don't leave your success up to chance. Be deliberate in making it happen by making it happen on schedule!

CREATE A BETTER YOU!
KEEP THE MAIN THING THE MAIN THING

FOCUS! FOCUS! FOCUS! That needs to be Habit #1! Learning to keep the main thing the main thing will make your life so much easier in the long run. If you're an "idea" person like me then you battle with having more ideas in your mind than time to work through them. It's easy to get distracted from the main priority while trying to engage in other seemingly equal important tasks and projects. You fool yourself into believing your diverse efforts are a positive thing because you're covering more ground, when in actuality, most times that's not the case.

Spreading yourself too thin leads to a little bit being done on several tasks but never fully completing any of them. You end up with a bunch of "good enoughs" and never any real "excellence". Forcing yourself to see a single project all the way through from inception to completion without engaging in any other project is going to be tough but so worth it in the long run. I saw a video online once of Tyler Perry speaking on this very topic. In his video he talked about how he put everything he had into his first play and worked solely on that production for three years until finally it took off. It wasn't until after his first play began to see the success he wanted that he began to put his efforts towards his next project.

I'm speaking from experience when I say this one is tough. I've had times when I was literally all over the place with ideas and just trying to do them all and see what would stick. Fortunately for me, the ideas all lined up with the same purpose but looking back I can see how that would be confusing for a consumer trying to figure out just who IS Ryan C. Greene? I knew the things I wanted to do but I had to slow down and exercise patience in developing my brand in the right order if I wanted to maximize my efforts. It's been a long difficult road but after seven years of writing books, I am finally ready to transition to the next phase in building my company, GreeneHouse Media.

12 ESSENTIAL ELEMENTS FOR YOUR GREATEST COMEBACK EVER!

For me that means it's time to develop new habits all over again. The habits of an author aren't the same as the habits of a film director. As I prepare to put down the pen and pick up the camera lens, the things I do will change and who I become will also change. For you I hope you choose to change the things you do so that your habits can make you the better person you want to be.

CREATE A BETTER YOU!
Journal

Chapter Notes:

_____
_____
_____
_____
_____
_____
_____
_____

I Need To Create Better Habits By:

_____
_____
_____
_____
_____

12 ESSENTIAL ELEMENTS FOR YOUR GREATEST COMEBACK EVER!

_____

_____

_____

Action Steps:

_____

_____

_____

_____

_____

_____

_____

_____

_____

CREATE A BETTER YOU!

Chapter Six

Create Better

COMMUNICATION

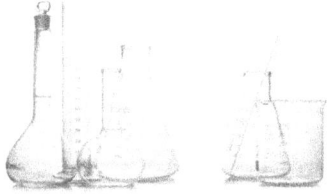

"Communication is Key." Who hasn't heard that saying a million times? But what does that even mean? Why does it seem like communicating what makes great effective communication is so hard to do? Everyone knows it sounds good and it's the right thing to say, yet very few have mastered great communication in all areas of their lives. Very few are great at all forms of communication.

Communication happens on three major levels- written, verbal, and nonverbal communication. Sometimes you may find someone who is an excellent writer however their verbal communication leaves much to be desired. You may find another person who speaks well and can move a crowd with their words, yet struggles to write in an equally persuasive way. Even still you may find someone who writes well and may even have great delivery but their body language is all off causing the message to get lost.

12 ESSENTIAL ELEMENTS FOR YOUR GREATEST COMEBACK EVER!

So what traits make someone great at the three levels of communication? Let's start with written communication. We're living in the world of "statuses" and "140-character tweets" so finding great written communication is becoming more and more difficult; however, it's still very important and necessary in becoming a better you and creating a better life. Bosses, business owners, and bankers don't speak "Twitter-ese". Business plans don't get funded when they include "LOL" or get signed "TTYL". Knowing how to present your ideas in a persuasive, clear and concise written manner is still critical to success in the real world.

When focusing on improving your written communication, here are five tips from a blog written on www.gigaom.com to help you create better written communication.

1) **Use precise language.** Stay away from vague words which may lead to ambiguity in your writing. Also, stay away from using jargon or industry specific words and abbreviations if your audience is outside of the industry.
2) **Keep your sentences short.** The longer your sentences are, the easier it is for readers to lose track. Error on the side of less is more when dealing with sentence length.
3) **Re-read what you've written.** Spell check only finds misspelled words but it doesn't catch misused words. You don't want to type "tore" when you meant "tour". Re-reading will also prevent you from becoming a victim of the Auto-Correct Monster. There's nothing worse than knowing you typed one thing only to press send and see your computer or smart phone changed your word to something else!
4) **Ask for feedback.** My belief is that it is the responsibility of the writer to convey their thoughts in a way that the reader "gets it". If people aren't readily following your written thoughts then it may be time to ask them for help in getting you to better explain yourself in your writing.

CREATE A BETTER YOU!

5) **Read messages out loud to yourself.** Reading what you've written out loud is a great way to make sure what you've written makes sense. It also can help make sure your words convey the message you're really trying to send. People can't read inflection and accent on words so make sure your words send the right message as if a monotone computer program were reading it to your reader.

Next there's verbal communication. This form of communication can make or break you in about the first 7 words out of your mouth. It doesn't take long for others to decide whether they are going to commit their attention to you and believe what you are saying. You have about 15 seconds to grab someone's attention and make them lock-in to hear more. Seems as if everyone has something to say but only those who say it the best will ever get heard and listened to. Here are 5 elements you must focus on in order to help you create better verbal communication:

1) **Words.** Sounds simple enough but how many times have you heard someone just flat-out use the wrong word in a sentence? Or use words that are too elementary or too abstruse for the audience? Or get blank stares from an audience who doesn't understand your regional slang which is foreign to them? Choose your words wisely and make sure they tell the story you intend to tell.

2) **Dialect and Accent.** This is a difficult one to overcome if you are used to speaking a certain way all your life however dialect and accent play a huge role in how your communication is received. While southern accents are traditionally seen as more trustworthy, they are also seen as less intelligent. Speaking in your "home" voice may work when at home but could backfire when speaking in other areas. You don't have to totally hide who you are but be cautious of how others may respond to your accent.

12 ESSENTIAL ELEMENTS FOR YOUR GREATEST COMEBACK EVER!

3) **Voice.** Now here is one that you really can't control. You either have a voice people enjoy hearing or you don't. Your voice plays a huge role in your verbal communication obviously because that's how people hear your words. I'm sure there are offerings out there to help people work on their actual voice but I'd say your unique voice is part of what makes you YOU so learn to embrace your voice and use it to your best ability.

4) **Tone.** Ever heard that saying "It's not what you say but how you say it."? That's what tone is. Tone is the how you say it and in verbal communication the tone is even more important than the actual words. Which words you stress in a sentence and how you emote your words construct the tone to your verbal communication and really determine how your words will be received by the listener. Make sure your tone reinforces the message you are trying to send through your words.

5) **Speed.** No one likes or trusts a fast talker. No one likes a super slow talker either. Finding the right speed for your audience is crucial in reaching them on a level where they will trust you and what you're saying. Learning to gauge your speed of communication as well as being able to sense what speed your listener is most comfortable with will help you communicate better.

Finally there's the most used form of communication, which coincidentally is also the most subconscious and ignored form, nonverbal communication. One of my mentors, Jeff Olson, author of <u>The Slight Edge</u>, calls this your "music". It's the language that shows not through your words, but through your actions and body movements. It's your aura. It's your charisma. It's your IT Factor. Long before the first words even come out of your mouth, your non-verbal communication, your "music", has already started telling your story.

Here are just a few aspects of nonverbal communication from About.com for you to recognize and work on:

CREATE A BETTER YOU!

1) **Facial Expression.** Saying "I love you" with a smile versus with a frown changes the entire meaning of the phrase. Stand in front the mirror and look at your face. Videotape yourself giving your presentation and look at the facial expressions you make. The camera doesn't lie. What it sees, your audience sees.
2) **Gestures.** Deliberate movements such as waving and pointing will help communicate your points in tandem with your words. Gestures can help drive home certain points where words may not be enough.
3) **Paralinguistics.** This is the vocal communication separate from actual words. Tone, loudness, inflection, and pitch would fall under this category. There's a reason why people yell "FIRE!!" and not whisper it during an emergency.
4) **Body language and posture.** Our body language and posture can indicate our true feelings and attitudes about what we're saying or hearing. While sometimes quite subtle in nature, body language and posture often times gives insight into how open or defensive one is to the message or messenger.
5) **Eye contact.** No eye contact at all makes you look shifty and untrustworthy. Long intense glares with minimal blinking makes you look like a psychopath. Find a comfortable middle ground when communicating with others and make frequent, but not creepy, eye contact.
6) **Touch.** In the dating world there's all kind of rules on how to tell if a woman likes you based on how many times she touches you while conversing. Sometimes people are just touchy feely types and other times touch is a great nonverbal clue as to how well a conversation is going.
7) **Appearance.** Let's be honest, people DO judge human books by their covers. Your appearance plays a significant role in your nonverbal communication. What you wear and how you style your hair impact greatly how your message will be received by others. A CEO in skinny jeans just isn't going to

demand the same level of respect as a CEO in a Brooks Brothers suit would.

So which area of communication do you need to work on most? Where are you going to first start creating better communication in your life? Communication is something every single one of us does every single day whether we want to or not. It's probably our single greatest activity yet it probably goes most undeveloped. If you want a better life, you must **CREATE BETTER COMMUNICATION**.

BE ABLE TO ARTICULATE YOUR THOUGHTS IN A CLEAR, CONCISE, CARING WAY

I live by the belief that it's always the communicator's fault if his or her message is not understood. If there's a misunderstanding, the blame first lies on the shoulders of the person attempting to convey the message. It's your responsibility to know your audience, know their level of understanding of the subject and relay it to them in the best way for them to understand what message you are conveying.

First, be CLEAR. Clarity is King in communication. Make it clear what exactly you are trying to convey. Nothing frustrates me more than trying to listen to someone stumble over their words, start over three times, or switch conversation topics halfway through the first convo. If at the end of you talking, people are looking at you more confused than when you started, somewhere along the way you lost the clarity game.

Next, be CONCISE. Women are notoriously known for being ramblers; however, this trait isn't gender specific. Have you ever been listening to someone speak and it took everything in you not to yell "Get to the point!!"? If you want people to pay attention to you and remain fully engaged in what you are saying, at some point you have to shut up. If someone asks you a question you need to learn when

CREATE A BETTER YOU!

you should lead with the story and then answer or answer first and then follow-up with the story if need be. You don't want to be that person who everyone avoids your calls and office visits because you simply talk too much and never get to the point.

Finally, you need to be CARING. In communicating with others you will always get a much better response from those who feel like you care about them. If you're the type who has to lead every statement with "I don't mean any harm but..." you are probably not showing enough care toward the people to whom you speak. "I'm just keeping it real" is not an excuse for you to berate people with mean hurtful words. Only thing you're going to be doing is keeping it real ignorant, rude, and disrespectful. Get over yourself and begin caring more about the person on the other side of the conversation and watch how much more effective your words will become.

WHO ARE YOU AND WHY SHOULD OTHERS CARE?

If someone were to ask you "Who are you?" how would you respond? Not "What's your name?" or "What do you do for a living?" but WHO are you? How would you answer that question? When you think about it, who are you really? That's a question we each need to be able to answer for ourselves. We need to know who we are and then live by that and be able to convey that to others.

So who ARE you? What do you represent? What do you value in life? What is your purpose for being created? What motivates you? Where does your passion lie? WHO you are is much more than your title at work. It's much more than what you do for a living or at home. Who you are is all about what contribution you are making to the world. So take a minute now and ask yourself "Who AM I?" Match that answer up with who you wish to be and if they do not match, you have some work to do.

12 ESSENTIAL ELEMENTS FOR YOUR GREATEST COMEBACK EVER!

After you've defined WHO you are, you then need to define WHY others should care about that. Why is it important to them that you are who you are? In the context of communication this is important so that others can decide where you fit into their own lives. You need to communicate to others what value you will bring them because of who you are. This should never be done in an arrogant "you need me" kind of way, but when you can communicate your value properly to the right people, they will have no choice but to want you around.

Getting people to care about who you are and thereby seeing a need to have you around is best done through actions. If you have to continually *tell* someone you are valuable, then you are not spending enough time *showing* them your value. Who you are should show through the actions you take. You can run down a litany of characteristics you wish to possess; however, the only traits that matter are the ones you consistently truly display. Who you are shows through your actions every time.

MAKE PEOPLE R.A.V.E. ABOUT YOU

The best form of communication when it comes to you growing your personal brand is 3rd party verification in the form of mouth-to-mouth endorsements. You want to be that person everyone raves about when your area of expertise is brought up. You want to position yourself as the go-to person in your field. Here are four qualities you must have in order to make others R.A.V.E. about you.

RELEVANCE- The first thing you must bring to any relationship and communication is relevance. There has to be a need for you and your message. If you are an expert on picture tube televisions in the current world of flat screen HD LED TV's then you are irrelevant. It doesn't matter how much you know about your subject, if it has no impact on present matters then no one will listen. One big pitfall

CREATE A BETTER YOU!

"experts" fall into is not being able to keep current with their industry so that their message remains relevant and needed.

AUTHENTICITY- People can smell a salesman a mile away. They can smell authenticity too. I believe it's OK to be a copycat as long as you're copying the right cat, but stop trying to be like everyone else. Find your own voice and message that speaks to you first before you try to share it with everyone else. Don't worry about being the best [insert what you want to be here]. Only concern yourself with being the best YOU. Don't get caught up with every new Flavor of the Month that comes along. Stay true to yourself and let your authenticity sell you.

VALUE- There's an entire chapter on creating more value later in this book but understand that the more value you bring to a relationship, the more difficult it is for others to replace you. If you focus on being more valuable by being the best at what you do then people will have no choice but to rave about you to others. Don't be overly concerned with what you're getting out of every interaction. Instead concern yourself first with how much value you're bringing to the interaction.

EXCITEMENT- Here's a little secret- The more excited you get about whatever it is you're talking about; the more excited people will be to listen. It's like magic; only it's real. Excitement is contagious! If you want folks to get excited, you have to get excited first. More times than not people will follow your excitement before they even follow your words. While you're spending all that time crafting the perfect message, make sure you spend enough time crafting the perfect delivery as well.

So for the million and first time, "Communication is Key". Know what you are saying out of your mouth as well as through your body language and actions. Take charge of your message and convey it the way you intend to. Say what you mean to say! Mastering the art of communication will not only make your life better but the lives of those to whom you're communicating better too. If you want or need more out of life, you need to know how to communicate that need to those who are able to give it to you.

CREATE A BETTER YOU!
Journal

Chapter Notes:

_____

_____

_____

_____

_____

_____

_____

_____

_____

I Need To Create Better Communication By:

_____

_____

_____

_____

_____

12 ESSENTIAL ELEMENTS FOR YOUR GREATEST COMEBACK EVER!

_____

_____

_____

Action Steps:

_____

_____

_____

_____

_____

_____

_____

_____

_____

CREATE A BETTER YOU!

Chapter Seven

Create Better

RELATIONSHIPS

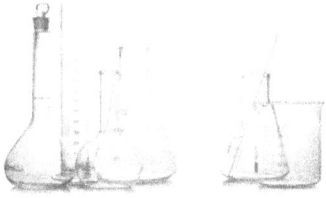

In 1987 my mother purchased her first home. It was a townhouse in the Rockdale/Randallstown area of Baltimore County, MD. It was a new community so only a few families were living there when we first moved in. As more families moved in, there were plenty of kids in the neighborhood and we all became close pretty quickly. Most of us who grew up on Western Winds Circle still keep in touch today thanks to the advent of social media.

We all knew each other. My god-mother's sister lived next door to us. One of my best friends to this day, Derrick Hamlin, lived directly across the street. Next to him lived one of my sister's best friends. Next to them lived one of my mother's co-workers. Next to them lived Miss Alice. Everybody knew and loved Miss Alice. Miss Alice had five kids of her own but she also ran a day care and sold ice cream from her basement.

12 ESSENTIAL ELEMENTS FOR YOUR GREATEST COMEBACK EVER!

All of Miss Alice's kids were older than me but I went to school with her two youngest. Her middle son, Omar, was already in high school when I was in middle school so while we weren't "friends" in the sense of hanging out and growing up together, we both knew one another. I would always see him walking to and from school with a briefcase or something that made him look like he was all about business. By the time I was in high school, he was in college and by the time I went away to college I don't know where he was. 1993 was the last time I remember seeing Omar on a regular basis in the neighborhood.

Fast forward 12 years to 2005. I had just finished writing my first book **Success Is In Your Hand: 19 Keys To Unlocking The Successful Person You Were Designed To Be** and was looking for media avenues to promote my book. Who do I run into at a networking event? You guessed it, my old neighbor, Omar Muhammad. Come to find out, Omar was the Director at Morgan State University's Entrepreneurial Development Assistance Center and hosted a weekly radio show on Morgan's radio station WEAA 88.9FM. Every week he had the ear of thousands of people in my target market. We discussed my book and he agreed to have me on his show for an interview to spotlight my book. That was my first radio interview ever.

Omar didn't stop extending a hand to me at that radio interview. Within that same year Omar offered me an opportunity to be a stand-in host for his show! I had become a regular guest, but now he was offering me an opportunity to sit as HIS mic and actually host a show for him. Talk about being excited and discovering a new passion! There I was, someone who had always loved and dreamt of being on the radio but had no formal training, now being offered a chance to host a radio show in my home town. Omar went from being the man who granted me my first radio interview to now becoming the man who gave me my first radio hosting gig all in a matter of one year. But that was just the beginning.

CREATE A BETTER YOU!

In 2007, Omar embarked upon a new project; a television talk show on Morgan's TV Station. Who does he invite on as his first guest on the show? ME! I had never done a television interview but you better believe I accepted the offer! Television was such a different animal since now people could see me. Hosting my own TV Talk Show was my goal so this was just another step in that direction to me. I still remember the suit, shirt and tie I wore to the taping. Being on the set was exhilarating. Seeing my dreams come to life was amazing. There I was now the "expert" on a TV Show.

So what happens next? Eventually, Omar needed someone to fill in for him to host the TV Show and he once again called on the kid from 'round the way' to help him out. So in a matter of two short years one man gave me my first radio interview, my first radio host position, my first television interview and my first television talk show hosting opportunity. When you're in the middle of living your dreams sometimes the gravity of the situation and how impactful the actions of others are on your future can go unnoticed. When I sat down to write this chapter on relationships it only felt right to give proper shine to the man who took so many chances on an unproven Ryan.

Sure I wrote the book that put me in position to take advantage of the opportunity, but I called many talk show hosts who all shut the door in my face. Why did Omar give me that first shot and so may after that? It was all about our relationship we built 12 years prior. He remembered that kid from the neighborhood and he looked out for me. The first door was opened based on our previous relationship. After that, he saw I was professional and knew what I was doing and talking about so a new relationship began to form leading to all of the subsequent opportunities. When I started hosting my own radio show **"The Ryan C. Greene Show"** in 2007, the first guest I had on was none other than Omar Muhammad.

I'm a firm believer in that saying "It's not *what* you know, but *who* you know." But I like to add the caveat "...and how they feel about you." You better know your stuff if you want to be put in any position of significance, but you also better know the right people. Still more important than knowing the right people is the relationship you have with those people. When someone of influence hears your name what kind of response is triggered in their mind about you? If you were job searching and your old college roommate was the HR Professional making the hiring decision, what would they say and think if your resume' came across their desk?

I know when in the heat of the moment and faced with the opportunity to give someone a piece of their mind most people don't think about the effects their decisions today may have on their lives 15 years down the line. The next time you get ready to burn a bridge though, you better ask yourself if that 10 seconds of unfiltered rant or that terrible tweet to put someone "on blast" is worth you losing any and all future influence you may have in that person's life. Emotion is natural but you cannot afford to fly off the handle and let it get the best of you and destroy relationships with other people. A big key to creating a better you is to **CREATE BETTER RELATIONSHIPS.**

TREAT PEOPLE TODAY AS IF...

How would you treat someone today if you knew that 10 years from now you would have to ask them for 10 Million Dollars? Would you be so quick to curse them out when they upset you next time? Would you smear their name all over social media sites for the sake of "keeping it real" to get revenge for something they did to you? How you respond to and interact with people today could have huge impacts on your life in the future. There's an old saying about not burning bridges because you never know when you may need to cross them again. I wish more people thought about that before they went flying off the handle.

CREATE A BETTER YOU!

In my story it was a radio interview from someone I had a positive interaction with 12 years prior. For you it may be a former co-worker who ends up being HR Director at a company you're applying to 10 years from now. That singer you kicked out the group without so much as a phone call and explanation could end up becoming Program Director at the very station you've been trying to get to play your new single. Your ex-girlfriend could go on to become a doctor and deliver you and your current wife's baby. You just never know how things are going to go so it's important you treat each person as if they are potentially a decision maker on a $10 Million Deal for you.

This doesn't mean you go around using people and building fake relationships in hopes of getting a big payoff in the future. What I'm saying is focus on building genuine relationships and treating people with the respect you would hope to be given. Control your emotions in uncomfortable situations so that they never come back to bite you and prevent you from bigger and better things down the line. The instant gratification of getting something off your chest right now, may ultimately prevent you from living that better life you seek down the line.

LEARN TO FORGIVE

I truly believe that a super majority of the pain, heartache, stress, and drama people experience in their lives is there simply because they have not learned to forgive. People spend more time focused on how someone else did them wrong and how they are going to seek revenge on that person for how they hurt them than they spend focused on how they can simply let it go and move on. Forgiveness is your most powerful weapon! The freedom attained from simply letting go is life changing. Past pains have no power once you have truly forgiven the inflictor of the pain.

For some reason people have come to equate forgiveness with weakness. They seem to feel like forgiving someone means you've lost the battle. I look at forgiveness as the exact opposite. When you can forgive someone of the hurt they caused you, you negate any power they once had over you from your harboring of the negative feelings and energy caused by their actions. If GOD can forgive each of us for the plethora of sins we commit daily, and still love us enough to sacrifice His only Son so that we may still have everlasting life with Him in Heaven, then who are you to think you cannot bring yourself to forgive that humanly person for ANYTHING they may have done to hurt you? Get over yourself and get to forgiving!

Stop letting simple arguments ruin great relationships. All people really want to know in an argument is "Did you hear me and did anything I said matter to you?" If we spent less time yelling and more time listening during discussions of disagreement we'd also spend less time mending broken relationships. Sometimes arguments happen, not because someone is trying to be right, but they're simply trying to be heard. They're tired of being ignored and their voice lost in the noise. They want to know that they matter to you. When you can learn to shut up and listen to the other voices in your relationships and value those voices as much as your own, you will find your relationships begin to grow exponentially deeper as others become more comfortable in trusting you with their thoughts and vulnerabilities.

PEOPLE ARE YOUR MOST VALUABLE RESOURCE AND ASSET

I don't know how many times I've said it in this book but if you haven't figured out by now that people are the most valuable resource you can access, you should start over reading from Chapter 1. There's no getting away from that fact. None of us live in a vacuum or inside of

CREATE A BETTER YOU!

our own self-contained bubble. We need each other to survive and thrive so how we relate to one another is most important. The more people you have on your team, in your circle, at your disposal, the more valuable YOU are to others. Why do you think every author wanted to be on Oprah's Book Club List? Why do people make such a big deal over how many Twitter Followers people have? Why are companies like Klout sprouting up to rank your social media influence? It's because you're only as valuable as the people you know.

Knowing people isn't good enough. How those people feel about you is where the true value lies. You can round-up thousands of people who will at least pay attention to what you have to say, but if you don't touch them or make them feel like more than dollar signs in your eyes, then you just lost those same thousands of people. You have to touch people and build real relationships, real connections. We live in the day and age where we send mass text messages for everything from Holiday Greeting to Birth and Death Announcements. Try this novel idea- CALL instead of text. You may be amazed at just how impactful that once normal gesture can be on building relationships since it's now out of the norm.

The minute you begin taking people for granted you will begin to see your relationships suffer because of it. Don't focus so much on quantity, but make quality your goal. It's much easier to get $10 out of one happy client 10 times than it is to find 10 new clients to give you $10 each. Foster your relationships and give even more than you receive. Before you ask someone to do something for you, find something you can do for them first. No one likes a leech that uses people for money grabs. You first be the person to others you want others to be to you.

Relationships don't have to be difficult if you keep a few things in mind:

1) Only get into relationships with people you genuinely care about.

12 ESSENTIAL ELEMENTS FOR YOUR GREATEST COMEBACK EVER!

2) Be open and honest within your relationships.

3) Be fair and equitable not expecting more than you are willing to give yourself.

4) Know when to it is time to end relationships no matter how good or bad it is.

5) Understand that you cannot get into every relationship presented to you.

6) Loyalty in relationships is top priority.

7) Allow room for personal growth among those in the relationship.

Keep these tips in mind and you will be creating better relationships in no time.

CREATE A BETTER YOU!
Journal

Chapter Notes:

_____

_____

_____

_____

_____

_____

_____

_____

I Need To Create Better Relationships By:

_____

_____

_____

_____

12 ESSENTIAL ELEMENTS FOR YOUR GREATEST COMEBACK EVER!

_____

_____

_____

Action Steps:

_____

_____

_____

_____

_____

_____

_____

_____

_____

CREATE A BETTER YOU!

Chapter Eight

Create Better

DECISIONS

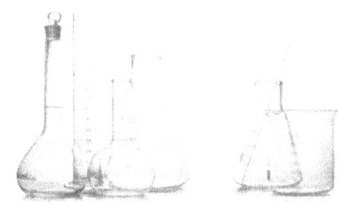

Where you are today is the result of decisions you made five years ago. The decisions you make in your life affect not only you, but those around you. Your family, friends, co-workers, neighbors and even strangers are counting on you making better decisions in order to make everyone's life better. If it's true that you learn from your mistakes; then it is also true that if you want to create a better life then you must **CREATE BETTER DECISIONS.**

I want to talk about two types of decisions that will affect your life and how to improve your decision-making in both. First, there are those decisions that determine what you DO. I'll call those "DO-cisions". Secondly, there are those decisions that determine who you ARE. I'll call those "YOU-cisions". Decisions that determine what you DO, DO-cisions, are decisions that elicit a physical or tangible response. They can range from something as simple as whether or not to speak to a passerby to something huge like what kind of home to purchase. The who you ARE decisions, YOU-cisions, deal with the intangible aspects of life and affect how you are viewed in the eyes of others. Ironically, the decisions you make in one category usually also impacts the other. If you don't speak to that passerby that can either negatively or positively impact how they feel about you.

How do you create better decisions in relation to what you do? Surely we have all faced times when we have had to make decisions on how to handle a situation. We've had to decide just how important is our reputation, just how important is our career and even just how important is our freedom, if someone cuts us off in traffic. Some people make good decisions and reap the rewards of such. Others make poor decisions and suffer the consequences just the same. Here are my suggestions on making better "DO-cisions".

Evaluate your goals and how they pertain to each decision. Keeping your ultimate goal of every interaction in the forefront of your mind is key to making sure the situation goes in a way most beneficial to you. Things may not always go the way you desire however if you understand your goals you have a better chance of making decisions that will be best for you even if they hurt a little bit.

Weigh all possible outcomes. Once you have your goal in mind you must then weigh all the possible outcomes of the scenario. Taking time to do this prevents you from making emotional and impulsive decisions. You then want to compare each possible outcome with your goals from Step 1. You can quickly eliminate options that do not line up with your goals for the particular scenario.

Think about how your decision will affect others. Remember that although it's ultimately your decision to make, there are other people affected by your choice. Only a selfish person puts only their needs into consideration when making any decision. If your decision will negatively impact those closest to you then that may not be the best choice to make.

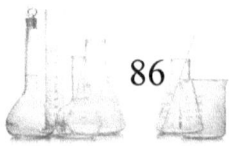

CREATE A BETTER YOU!

Decide which consequences you are willing to live with. This part of the decision-making process is where most average people get tripped up. Most people are so used to simply acting on how they feel right now that they never consider how the consequences of their actions will impact them in years to come. Whether it is a criminal not thinking about the years behind bars they'll spend if they get caught or the cheating spouse not thinking about the lifelong repercussions from creeping with a jumpoff for even one night, if you can't live with the consequences of your decision don't choose that path!

Choose to do the right thing. Ultimately every decision you make is going to boil down to you simply choosing to do the right thing. You have to deliberately make the choice that for your better life you will make better/right choices. "Right" doesn't necessarily default to morally right (although that's preferred) but what is right for you and your situation based on the assessment you made during the decision-making process. You can never go wrong by choosing to do the right thing.

So how then do we make better YOU-cisions? How do we make sure our decisions match the person we think we are, want to be or want other to see? These decisions are based on the very makeup of our being. Once you begin making better YOU-cisions that will help you begin making better DO-cisions. There are three YOU-cisions you should make right away and every day:

Decide to be honest. Honesty is telling the truth BEFORE you get caught in the lie. As I stated earlier, people are your greatest resource. Influence is the currency of people capital. Trust is the greatest way to accumulate influence. Honesty begets trust. If you want people to trust you then you have to make the decision to be honest with them. How many times have you caught someone in a lie and only when you expose your evidence or smoking gun to them do they then admit guilt of wrongdoing? That's NOT honesty. That's getting caught. If you're the type of person who is only as honest as the evidence forces you to be then you need to change that if you honestly want to create a better life for yourself.

Decide to be of good character and high integrity. Character and integrity are not who you are when everyone is around and looking, but who you are and what you do when no one else is watching. Anyone can put on a show for an audience that makes them look like they live a clean life; but who are you when no one is watching? The real you is that person you see in the mirror when you're alone. The person who only you and God know what you're doing is the person your character and integrity is based on. Are you the same person or are you putting on airs? When no one is watching can you be trusted to still do the right thing? Character and integrity are so precious and so immensely difficult to rebuild that you'd be a fool to squander it on some nonsense. Yet we see it happen daily. Don't be that fool.

Decide to commit to excellence. Commitment is doing what you said you would do long after the excitement of the moment you said it in has passed. Excellence is a verb. It's the state of knowing that good enough is never good enough. To create a better you and a better life you have to decide to stop settling for mediocre and stop quitting. Average people live content and comfortable lives. They are happy with just getting by. But excellent people, the most successful people, the better person you want to become, strive to live a most fulfilled extraordinarily abundant life! They do that by making a decision to commit themselves to only accepting excellence in all they do.

DON'T LET YOUR CIRCUMSTANCES CONTROL YOUR CHARACTER

"Character" is defined by Merriam-Webster as: the mental and moral qualities distinctive to an individual. It's the distinctive nature of something. Character is a noun. Character doesn't describe you, like an adjective. Character isn't something you do, like a verb. Character is a thing. It is what and who you are. Your character is your distinct nature. It is made up of what you do, how you think and what you believe is right and wrong to make up You. Your character speaks for you when you are not around to speak for yourself. Your character is what drives your actions and decisions. Aspects of your character may change over time but your character itself is permanent.

Merriam-Webster defines "Circumstances" as facts or conditions connected with or relevant to an event or action. It's an event or fact that causes or helps to cause something to happen typically something undesirable. So our circumstances lead to certain events and actions. Negative circumstances don't necessarily lead to negative events, just as positive circumstances don't always lead to positive events. Circumstances change like the wind. We cannot always control our circumstances but we can, and must, control our responses to all of our circumstances. Circumstances are temporary.

As you embark on creating a better you, it is important to realize and accept that your circumstances right now is just what's going on right now. You cannot allow your temporary situations to affect your permanent character. Do not grow impatient during the process of creating a better you and end up going against your character by taking shortcuts that could lead to even worse results.

Emotions are not a bad thing. Allowing your emotions and how you feel in the heat of the moment to determine how you respond to circumstances could have much further reaching consequences on your future than you can fully evaluate at that time. No matter the circumstances, always lean on your character as your guide when it comes to making the proper decisions. Work to control your circumstances; don't let your circumstances control you.

12 ESSENTIAL ELEMENTS FOR YOUR GREATEST COMEBACK EVER!
GET HELP RIGHT AWAY

When I was married and things began going south for us, the biggest mistake we probably made was not getting help soon enough. I still believe we would have split regardless, but perhaps we wouldn't have felt so hopeless or each harbored so much pain and anger towards each other in the end. We both could see the wheels falling off, knew that neither of us was a marriage mechanic, yet we kept rolling along on four loose flats. Ultimately the inevitable happened and we split.

Hopefully divorce isn't what you are facing but certainly there's an area in your life where you are weak. There's something you need help fixing and up until this point you have been too ashamed to ask for help. I implore you to find the help you need right now. The only shame bigger than needing help is needing help, not asking for help then finding out how easy it would have been to get the help you needed after the fact.

As a man, I know how hard it is to battle that three-letter word "EGO" and accept that you are not Superman and some problems are simply too big for you to tackle alone. I understand the humbling feeling of going to someone and accepting your own shortcomings by asking for their help. But as a man, as an adult (male or female), it is your responsibility to make the best decisions for the overall success of your family and sometimes that decision is to get help.

So many times I have seen relatively small problems turn into huge catastrophes all because someone waited too late to ask for help. Pride will kill you. It will cause you to make stupid decisions just to hide your reality from others. What I've found in my experiences is that in the end, most people could care less about your shortcomings. Everyone is in the same boat trying to get ahead. Sometimes the very people you're trying to hide your dirt from are going through the same dirt and trying to find someone to help them through it. Start making better decisions. Stop hiding and start seeking the help you need right away.

GET INPUT FROM PEOPLE WHO ARE SMARTER THAN YOU

If you are the smartest person (or think you are) in your circle of friends then you need new smarter friends. If you are the Top Dog, "The Answer" among your friends then how is that helping you? How can you grow if you are The Lid? The best way to make the best decisions is through a collaborative meeting of minds from multiple disciplines and trainings. If you are the smartest person you know and only ever consult yourself on major decisions then there's no way you're making the best decisions each time.

Consulting people smarter than you doesn't mean you're dumb or less intelligent. The contrary is true. It means you're smart enough to realize you don't know everything there is to know about everything. More importantly, it also means you're smart enough to know where to find the experts who do know the answers. Leadership isn't about always knowing the answers. Leadership is about knowing where to find the answers.

If you are one of those people who does go to others for advice but you have a habit of asking the wrong people for advice than you to need to find people smarter than you for the advice you seek. You'll be hard pressed to find any valuable marriage advice from someone who's proclaimed to be a lifelong playa and never been married sporting a new girlfriend every 3 months. I wouldn't go to an auto mechanic for advice on installing my office's computer network. Who you ask is just as important than what you're asking.

If you want spiritual advice, ask someone with a strong spiritual foundation with a reputation of studying and applying the doctrine they follow. I wouldn't ask an English teacher for help with my math

12 ESSENTIAL ELEMENTS FOR YOUR GREATEST COMEBACK EVER!

problems. If you want to create a better life for yourself, you're going to have to start making better decisions. Your decisions directly impact your circumstances. Find people in your life with a track record of making good decisions and make them your new circle. It will be one of the best decision you ever make.

CREATE A BETTER YOU!
Journal

Chapter Notes:

_____

_____

_____

_____

_____

_____

_____

_____

I Need To Create Better Decisions By:

_____

_____

_____

_____

12 ESSENTIAL ELEMENTS FOR YOUR GREATEST COMEBACK EVER!

_____

_____

_____

Action Steps:

_____

_____

_____

_____

_____

_____

_____

_____

CREATE A BETTER YOU!

Chapter Nine

Create Better

FINANCES

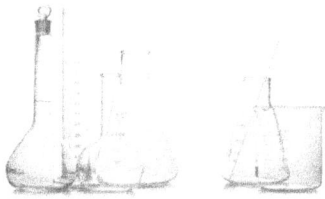

It's time to talk about money. What kind of feelings do you get when you think about your personal finances? Can you look at your financial situation and be proud of decisions you've made and where you currently stand financially? What would you do differently? Does money scare you? What is your personal attitude toward money and what its purpose is in your life? If you have negative responses to any of these questions then it's time for you to **CREATE BETTER FINANCES**.

How do most people first learn about finances and money management? Most of our first financial teachers are our parents. We watch how they manage the family budget and we either copy them or do the exact opposite of what we see them do. If parents stressed over money and pinched every penny then more than likely their children grew up to be penny pinchers, or depending on how they processed the results of their parent's money management skills, they may have taken the opposite route and become careless about their money management.

Growing up I watched my mother struggle financially and live check to check. Even though she made a great salary at her "good gub'mint" job; she overspent, over extended her credit, and was often behind on her bills. Regardless of her poor money management she always found a way to make ends meets somehow. She always found a way to afford the things she wanted even if it meant paying more important bills late. That was my financial education. Spend what you want and find a way to pay for it later. Once I got to college, it only took one free Snickers Bar and a water bottle to begin my downward financial spiral.

I don't know why colleges allowed credit card companies to post up on campuses and prey on unknowing, unemployed, uneducated, broke college students and lure them into credit slavery but that's what happened to me and so many others. I still remember it like it was yesterday even though it was 1995. There was a table set up right outside the cafeteria on campus and they were giving away free candy bars, water bottles and other gifts for everyone who applied for a Visa Card that day. Of course I applied and for some reason they approved a non-working, no income having college junior and gave me "free money".

The credit card didn't come with any literature on what credit was. It didn't come with any warnings on the impact credit would have on me once I actually needed it. It didn't come with any financial literacy classes on how to be prudent with my credit. It just came with a credit limit of $500 and an "ACTIVATE NOW" sticker which may as well read "SHOPPING SPREE!" because that's what I did. I used that credit card to buy some new clothes and when that card reached its limit, I applied for a Macy's Card and bought MORE clothes. Then the bill showed up in the mail.

CREATE A BETTER YOU!

There I was with still two more years before graduating college and I was already facing the Bad Credit Monster. I was already in credit card debt and I hadn't even applied for my first job yet. No one at school explained to me how bad credit could impact the jobs I would be able to have, the places I would be able to live or how much I'd pay for a mortgage or car note. I graduated college with the "B.C." (Bad Credit) Scarlet Letter on my Equifax Report all for a darn candy bar. I was already behind, and literally paying the price for it, before I could even begin my career.

Eventually I was forced to clean up my old credit when I bought my first home. Buying a house was a pain with all the hoops they put you through but it was ultimately a blessing to finally be forced to pay off that old debt. Having the foot of "the man" off my throat was a relief- although short-lived. Shortly after buying my home I joined network marketing. I had moderate success early on and was on my way to building a very successful business until I made one bad decision that messed up everything. I decided to quit my job.

The problem wasn't that I quit my job. There were quite a few successful full-time associates in my company. The problem was that I quit my job too soon! I was wrapped up in the dream, wrapped up in the hype and success I was having and wrapped up in the joy I'd get from firing my boss. I was miserable at work and I wanted to be the next Associate to proudly proclaim my freedom by leaving my job to work from home. The problem was: 1) I wasn't ready in many ways to go full-time 2) my business wasn't big enough yet to sustain my lifestyle 3) I had no back-up plan or nest egg to support me and 4) I didn't have the support of my wife at the time.

The first thing I noticed once I went full-time into my business was that my stress level rose tremendously. Building my business was no longer fun, but something I HAD to do. It was my only option. I still had success but as the bills began to mount and since I was making less money than I was making at my job, things began to spiral downward again financially. I put my family under stresses that as a husband I never should have allowed and eventually that, on top of many other things, led to our breaking point and ultimately our divorce.

I knew I had to do something different. I knew I needed to change how I managed my finances in order to ensure my future would be different from my past and present. Something had to give to make sure I could actually live the lifestyle I was chasing and had always dreamed about. I knew deep inside that God had not purposed me to live a life of lack and that my financial state was a direct representation of the poor decisions I previously made. All I needed was someone to show me how to do it, what to do with money once I had it, and I knew things would improve.

I began to search for financial teachers. I don't mean teachers as in school teachers but as in financial experts. That's when I found Robert Kiyosaki and Dave Ramsey. There are plenty of great financial experts and authors out there but these two really impacted me most and changed everything about how I viewed money. Robert Kiyosaki is the bestselling author of the **Rich Dad, Poor Dad** book series and his main teaching points involve understanding what real assets and liabilities are and how to create more income-earning assets in order to build true wealth. Dave Ramsey is the author of **Total Money Makeover** and his main teaching point is to live a CASH ONLY, DEBT FREE lifestyle. Many "gurus" talk about living debt free but Ramsey actually gives you a step by step roadmap to achieve it.

I don't want to share too much about the books because I would do the authors and you a grave disservice by giving you Cliff Notes, so I implore you to get the books and begin creating your better finances today. As I am still on my personal journey to reaching my financial goals, the main thing that has helped me keep sane along the way is the understanding of what money is, how to create it and most importantly how to no longer let it (or lack thereof) control me. If you

CREATE A BETTER YOU!

want a better life, you don't have to be rich but you DO have to gain better control of your finances.

EVERY DOLLAR SHOULD HAVE A JOB

How many times have you gone out and spent money or looked at your account at the end of the week and been clueless as to how you spent so much money? Or even worse, clueless as to what you spent it on? The biggest lesson Dave Ramsey teaches in **Total Money** Makeover is to budget every dollar every pay period. He doesn't leave anything to chance and forces you to give a job to every single dollar you earn. Even your disposable money needs to be accounted for in his system. It truly was an eye-opening lesson when I read the book.

Many of us simply waste money because it's in our pocket (or account). We really don't have a plan for our money after bills are paid so we spend as we see fit. Ramsey's system is all about getting debt-free and living a Cash Only lifestyle. It takes discipline and a paradigm shift to only buy what you can afford right now but it is the most financially freeing experience you will ever have. Saying no to credit cards and instant gratification in order to break free from the shackles of credit and debt is so worth it.

Not making enough money isn't always the problem for people in financial crisis. Not doing the right things with the money you have is usually the real problem. You can't spend $1,500 on a purse if you can't even afford to put $1,500 IN the purse on any given day. Instead of buying a brand new car with five years of payments that will instantly depreciate when you leave the showroom, buy a used car that you can pay off in a year instead. As I said, it's a paradigm shift. A change mentally to what you value. Which do you value more? Keeping up with The Jones' or financial freedom?

12 ESSENTIAL ELEMENTS FOR YOUR GREATEST COMEBACK EVER!

You don't have to make six-figures to put your money to work toward you getting debt-free. Ramsey's plan teaches you how to do it no matter your income level. It's really up to you how bad you really want your financial freedom. His is the only financial management book I recommend. His plan is simple, he educates you on many money myths and traps that keep us under the burden of debt and it works. Get the book and put your money to work.

EITHER SPEND LESS OR EARN MORE

When it comes to finances and balancing your budget, there are only two options to improving your bottom line. You can either spend less money or you can earn more money. That's it really. Look at Congress and that's what they fight over. The Republicans want to spend less money by cutting everything they feel is unnecessary and The Democrats want to earn more money by raising tax revenues. Neither side agrees with the other so the country's budget and finances go down to drain while they wrangle for power.

Let's start with spending less. This is probably the easier path to start with when you decide to create better finances for yourself. It's pretty simple to go line by line in your spending and cut out the waste. Cutting out Starbucks alone could save you over $35-$50 a week. Learning to cut your own hair, do your own nails, mow your own lawn are all ways you can immediately cut costs and save money. Do you really need every movie channel on cable? Just how many pairs of black boots does one woman need at a time? I'm sure we can all find areas in our budget where we are overspending for no good reason.

But how much is too much to cut? When does it shift from balling on a budget to living like a pauper? Financial Freedom is great but living like a minimalist broke person just to be debt-free kind of defeats the purpose. If you simply cut everything and live on bare

CREATE A BETTER YOU!

bones, sure you may not owe anyone but where's the lifestyle in that? Spending less helped you save money but there's another option.

The other option is a bit more difficult but you can always find a way to make more money. This is how folks get tricked into credit debt however. Instead of actually *making* more money, credit allows them to *borrow* more money and live like they made the money. Our entire financial system thrives on the hope that Americans will continue to resort to credit and spend more than they will ever earn. Instead of resorting to credit, you have a few options when it comes to making more money. You can earn more money from 1) winning the lottery/gambling 2) get a higher wage/salary 3) start a home-based business or 4) investment profits.

Earning more doesn't give you an excuse to live lavish and burn through your money. The extra money should be used to pay off more debt sooner and to begin saving. Good luck on winning the lottery or the jackpot at the slot machines. Depending on your job, getting a raise at work could take years and the increase could end up being nominal. Investing money is a real option but takes professional help to do it right, is unpredictable, and takes time to see significant returns. That leaves starting a home-based business. A home-based business is probably the best option for creating more income simply because: a) you work on your schedule b) you get to do something you enjoy and c) the tax breaks of owning a business also put more money in your pockets. I'll talk some more about building a home-based business in the next segment.

BUILD A FINANCIAL PLAN B

If the Economic Crash of 2008 wasn't a clear enough sign that you need to have a Financial Plan B for your household, then I don't know what more you need to see. A job alone, even a "good gub'mint job", is not as a safe a bet as it used to be in previous generations. Far too often people get caught putting all their eggs in one basket only to find out when it's too late that the basket has a hole in it. What's your plan if your job shut the doors tomorrow? How would you survive if you were pink-slipped this week?

The truth is that most Americans are $400 a month away from bankruptcy. One missed paycheck would send most homes into a financial whirlwind. How devastating would it be to wake up on Pay Day and that direct deposit not be there? So what's your backup plan? What's your Plan B to avoid getting caught in a financial mess? Don't have one? Most people don't. Most people never think it could happen to them so they never plan for the worst case scenario. But take this as your warning. If you want to create better finances, you can start by working on your Plan B right now.

I've worked two home-based businesses as both Plan A's and Plan B's at different times. I found companies that were already well established with a successful track record of providing services I could use and proudly stand behind as well as paying what they said they would pay when they said they'd pay it. What are your hobbies that you could turn into an extra profit center at home? What services could you provide that others would pay you for? Find something you enjoy doing, doing well and wouldn't mind doing for/with others and get started! You can't wait until you need your Plan B to start building it. Get on it now!

CREATE A BETTER YOU!
Journal

Chapter Notes:

_____

_____

_____

_____

_____

_____

_____

_____

_____

I Need To Create Better Finances By:

_____

_____

_____

_____

_____

12 ESSENTIAL ELEMENTS FOR YOUR GREATEST COMEBACK EVER!

_____

_____

_____

Action Steps:

_____

_____

_____

_____

_____

_____

_____

_____

_____

CREATE A BETTER YOU!

Chapter Ten

Create A Better

LEADER

In case you haven't caught on yet; if you want a better life, you must create a better YOU! One more way to create a better you is by becoming a better LEADER. Becoming a better leader has nothing to do with getting a promotion on your job. It has nothing to do with getting a new title. It has nothing to do with your boss, family, co-workers or subordinates. Leadership is not about a position but about a purpose. Leading others is a major part of leadership; however, the first person you must learn to lead is yourself.

All of my life I've been a leader. At 8 years old I was staying home alone after school until my mother got home from work. In high school I was the captain of the JV and Varsity football teams and starting QB my Senior Year. In college I was in the Student Leadership Program, a Resident Assistant, President of The Student Union Board, Senior Class President, an Officer in The Student Recruitment Team, as well as an Officer in my Fraternity. After college I began to take leadership roles in church, business, and other organizations. Even at times when I tried to sit back, I was thrust into leadership roles.

Being a leader is something that has always come naturally to me. Whether I had the title or position and people were "forced" to follow me or whether people simply adhered to John C. Maxwell's "Law Of E.F. Hutton" and flocked to my leadership, leading is something I've always done. But why is leadership important? When it comes to leadership the bottom line is that it has little to do with your title and everything to do with your influence. When you speak do people listen? When you move do people follow? When you call do people answer?

Leadership isn't only about where you stand, but what you stand for. You're only a leader if others are following so ask yourself the question "Why would anyone want to follow me?" To create a better life you must grow your influence among other people. Take a look at some of the greatest leaders and you will find they all share certain qualities:

Vision- The main purpose of a leader is to chart the course for the followers to go. A leader without a vision is no leader at all. Leaders not only have the vision but they are capable of relaying the vision to the people and getting them to buy into the vision.

Charisma- The young people call this "swag" but grown folks know it as charisma. Charisma is that unspoken energy that jumps off of great leaders that makes others want to be like them, be near them and excited to work with them. Some people have it naturally, others have to manufacture it, but the best leaders all have charisma.

Voice- Leaders must have something worth listening to if they expect others to follow. There has to be some cause, large or small, to rally people around in order to lead them. The best leaders are those who have found their authentic voice and become the mouthpiece for their message or cause.

CREATE A BETTER YOU!

***Influence*-** Influence is the ability to get people to do something they otherwise would not have done had you not encouraged them to do it. That IS leadership. If you cannot influence the behaviors of others, then no matter what your business card says, you are not a leader.

***Passion*-** Often times it's not what you say but how you say it that moves the most people to action. Your actions and commitment to a cause will also draw people more than any marketing material could. When you "become" your cause, when it's all you can talk about, when everything about you revolves around your goals, that's the passion needed to be a great leader.

***Purpose*-** A leader without a purpose is pointless. It's like an oxymoron. If you want to lead others then you should have a great purpose for doing so. I cannot think of one significant leader who didn't have a purpose to fulfill. Your purpose in leadership is what will make way for all you need to be successful.

Now take an honest inventory of yourself. Where do you need to grow in your leadership qualities? Be honest! It's OK to admit to your weak areas right now. That's the purpose of this book. If you want to be a better leader then you have to know in what areas you need growth. You have to take accountability and become a better leader of yourself first, grow on the inside first, and then you can begin to lead others. If you want a better life, you must **CREATE A BETTER LEADER**.

YOU CAN MAKE EXCUSES OR YOU CAN MAKE A WAY

You want to know the fastest way to wear on my patience? Start running off a bunch of lame excuses as to why you couldn't do what you said you were going to do. Weak people make excuses while strong people make a way. Anyone who's ever pledged a Black Greek Letter Organization knows their own version of the poem "Excuses".

12 ESSENTIAL ELEMENTS FOR YOUR GREATEST COMEBACK EVER!

Every chapter's version is slightly different however the message is all the same.

> "Excuses.
> Excuses are tools of the incompetent. They build monuments of nothingness and bridges to nowhere. Those who specialize in them seldom accomplish anything.
> Excuses."

There simply is no place in the life of successful leaders for excuses. Leaders find a way to make things happen. They never settle for good enough and they never let obstacles get in the way of them achieving their goals. If you want to be a better leader then you are going to have to put away your excuses and start making things happen.

I don't want you to confuse excuses with valid reasons. There's a difference in the two. Being late to an appointment because you got lost on the way is an excuse. Missing an appointment because you died in your sleep overnight is a valid reason. OK I was kind of kidding there. There are many more examples that are less extreme that I could have used but I think you get the point. Leaders are revered not by the number of stories they can tell about why they couldn't accomplish a task but by the number of obstacles they are able to overcome along the way. Leaders don't make excuses, they make a way!

DON'T GET CONSUMED WITH TRYING TO FIT IN

Do you remember as a baby, one of the first toys you received being some kind of shape toy where you had to put the correct shape in the right hole? Mine was a dump truck. Do you remember how frustrating it made you when no matter how hard you tried to force the star shape into the square hole; it just would not fit? You would cry and throw a tantrum because the "toy was broken" and eventually give up

CREATE A BETTER YOU!

and throw the whole truck at your little sister (Sorry, Stacie). I bet if someone were to buy you that same toy for Christmas this year you may ask "What the heck were they thinking buying me this baby toy?" But if that toy is only for babies, why as adults do we still play that same game with our lives?

We try to squeeze our "broke, bad credit, check to check finances" peg into a "lifestyles of the rich and famous" hole by spending more money than we earn. Or in an effort to appear more well off than we are, we continue to make poor financial decisions. Our youth try to squeeze their "suburbia raised, two parent household, six-figure income, private school educated" peg into a "I'm a drug dealing, high school dropout, gang banging 2 CHAAIIINZZ!!! thug from the hood" hole just because that stereotype is celebrated in mainstream media. Constantly we frustrate ourselves trying to fit into something that we are not. We overlook the blessings of what we have and the power of our story, all in an effort to fit in with the "in" crowd because we think they have it better than we do.

If you are looking to live a better life and be a better leader then you cannot expect to fit in. Followers fit in while Leaders break the mold. There's a reason you were made how you are. You were designed to stand out so that you could lead the way instead of falling in line. If a better life is what you strive to have; then following the crowd should never be your goal. Eighty percent of people simply go along to get along. Their life isn't necessarily bad, but it is probably of minimal significance to others. It's that 20% who stand out and make 80% of the world happen that you should strive to be like.

Be comfortable with who you are and what you bring to the table. Find the joy in being you and allow yourself to be the mold everyone else shoots to be like. With everyone else fighting to be like the next man and copy what's hot, it's actually much easier simply being your authentic self. There's much less competition there.

12 ESSENTIAL ELEMENTS FOR YOUR GREATEST COMEBACK EVER!
TAKE ACTION

Think about the many opportunities each of us is given to change the course of our life. Surely there have been plenty of circumstances that would have redirected our course and outcomes in life had we only stepped up instead of backed up, spoke up instead of shut up or showed up instead of given up. Too many people have their best dreams, ideas and life changing events tucked away under a "Not right now" pillow in their mind. If you want to propel yourself into the realm of great leadership then being able to take action is essential.

The difference between potential energy and kinetic energy is that potential energy is the energy stored up and kinetic energy is the actual energy in action and working. Your potential to become a successful leader is great, however, you must take action, or become kinetic, in order to access that potential. How much potential you have stored inside is not as important as how much of it you can bring out of you. All your hopes, dreams, promises, and plans don't mean a thing if you do not take action and work toward them.

It seems simple enough and like it would only make sense, but taking action is really where many weak leaders get hung up. People spend a lot of time and resources making plans but it takes courage and commitment to put those plans to work. It takes courage to make that first prospecting phone call or to write and implement that business plan. It takes guts to walk away from a comfortable job to pursue something new and uncertain, but taking action is the only way to overcome your fears of failure. I cannot promise you will not fail if you take action, but I can promise if you do not take action you will fail every time.

God is the Greatest Leader of all and he has not given us the spirit of fear and yet it is that very emotion that keeps people frozen in the land of "What-Ifs" afraid to step into their destiny. Taking action means you are going to have to get rid of your friends "Shoulda",

CREATE A BETTER YOU!

"Woulda" and "Coulda." Taking action means you are going to have to jump out of your comfort zone. Taking action also means you are going to have to deal with and overcome the bumps and bruises of life. Taking action means you have to "Just do it." The bottom line is, if you want to be a better leader then you have to DO something.

12 ESSENTIAL ELEMENTS FOR YOUR GREATEST COMEBACK EVER!

Journal

Chapter Notes:

_____
_____
_____
_____
_____
_____
_____
_____

I Need To Create A Better Leader By:

_____
_____
_____
_____
_____

CREATE A BETTER YOU!

_____

_____
_____
_____

Action Steps:

_____
_____
_____
_____
_____
_____
_____
_____
_____

12 ESSENTIAL ELEMENTS FOR YOUR GREATEST COMEBACK EVER!

CREATE A BETTER YOU!

Chapter Eleven

Create Better

VALUE

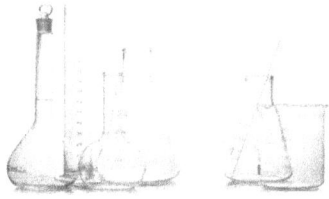

I was blessed to see the late Jim Rohn speak in Virginia Beach, VA in 2003. Jim Rohn is known as one of the world's greatest motivators and personal development coaches. At this particular workshop he was speaking on how to improve your value in the marketplace. He was sharing with the audience how important it was to differentiate yourself from the competition and stand out based on the value you bring to the table. Ten years later and I'm still sharing that same message everywhere I go.

What value do you bring to the table? Why would a company want to do business with you over someone else? Why would a love interest date you over any other fish in the sea? Why would your job promote you over your co-worker? The answers to those questions define your value. Quite honestly, most people don't have what they want in life because they don't bring enough value to the table to deserve the lifestyle they desire. If you want more, you have to bring more.

There's a good reason women want real diamonds in their engagement rings and not cubic zirconia. The diamonds have more value. I'd also venture to say there's a good reason some people want you in their lives and space while others do not. If you don't bring value to people's lives then the smart ones will remove you from their lives.

Want a better job? Bring more value to your employer.

Want a better love life? Bring more value to your relationships.

Want a better relationship with God? Bring more value to Him.

Want a better family? Bring more value to your spouse and kids.

Want better clients? Bring more value in your business offerings.

It all boils down to what you bring to the table. You may be the nicest person in the world, you may have all the money in the world, but if you don't bring enough value to the people you need in your corner, then you will find yourself in the corner alone. The easiest way to find out how you can bring the most value to a relationship is by simply asking that very question. "How can I be most valuable to this relationship?"

Sometimes people don't believe in you, not because they are hating on you, but because you haven't given them much to believe in. You haven't exhibited your full value to THEM. What may be valuable to one person in one type of relationship may not be as valuable to another person in a different setting. Finding out what is most valuable to each relationship is going to be your key to understanding what you are expected to bring to that relationship.

In Gary Chapman's book, _The 5 Love Languages_, he is ultimately discussing how to bring the most value to your relationship. The first book focuses on love/marriage relationships and he has another which focuses on parent/child relationships. Understanding how love languages are transferable to other relationships will help you create more value. Whether you are dealing with someone who values quality time, words of affirmation, gifts, acts of service or physical touch can be great information to have.

For example, if you're dealing with someone who values acts of service but you never do anything nice for them like pick up coffee on the way into the office or mow the lawn for your wife then your value to them will drop. If you never have anything nice to say to someone who values words of affirmation you will find yourself struggling to connect with them in a meaningful way. However, if you work with someone who values physical touch you may wanna call HR before things get out of hand! LOL.

Zig Ziglar said "People don't care how much you know, until they know how much you care about them." You want to increase your value? Start caring about more people more than you care about yourself. When you genuinely care about others, that caring shines through and people want to keep you around. More importantly, they will tell their friends and network about how valuable you are to them and begin to share your talents and skills with their networks. So if you want to improve your relationships and be the name everyone calls when they need what you do you must **CREATE BETTER VALUE**.

GET PAID FOR WHAT YOU KNOW; NOT FOR WHAT YOU DO.

One morning as I was deep in thought, I asked myself a question. I asked "Self, if you have a mind full of million dollar ideas, why are you still accepting pennies for your thoughts?" I had come to the realization that I was settling. I was settling for whatever I could get people to pay me for my knowledge all because of the circumstances I found myself in at the time. When you're facing losing your home, you're not really worrying about haggling over speaking or consulting fees. Sure I would LIKE to charge you my full speaking fee of $2,500 but if you only have $400 I'll take it! It seemed to make sense in the moment, but in the long run settling actually hurt me more than taking whatever fee people could afford. I was allowing groups to pay me for what I did when they should have been paying me for what I knew.

One important long-term investment every leader should make is an investment in education. I don't just mean formal school education but ongoing personal development and an investment into your mind for your entire life. Once your mind has been expanded it is impossible to shrink it back. It should be every leader's desire to learn as much about their field as possible and become an expert in it. The more you know the more valuable you become. That's why you want to move from getting paid for what you do to getting paid for what you know. You will always get paid more for what you know than for what you do.

How many times have you worked a job where it seemed as if you did all the work while your boss sat in their office doing seemingly nothing but they got paid more than you? Think about it, who gets paid more; the professional athlete or the team owner? Most professional athletes have played their sports all their lives, playing that game is all they have ever done and may be all they know how to do. The small percentage of athletes that reach the professional ranks are paid handsomely and live great lifestyles.

The team owner, on the other hand, more likely than not has never even played the sport of the team he or she owns but they know how to run a business. They know how to organize and run a profitable company and fit the many pieces together to make a successful organization. The athlete gets paid for what he does and the owner gets paid for what he knows. Not even New York Yankee, Alex Rodriguez makes more than The Steinbrenners.

CREATE A BETTER YOU!

No matter the field the same holds true. In education, the teachers get paid for what they *do* and the principal gets paid for what she *knows*. In music the singers gets paid for what they *do* and the label executives gets paid for what they *know*. Even lawyers and doctors get paid for what they *do* and judges and the surgeon general get paid for what they *know*. So if you want to get paid more you have to *learn* more not *do* more. Instead of doing more by working 10 hours overtime use that time to learn more, get a promotion and earn more.

Most people who complain about their job never say they hate what they *know*, they always hate what they *do*. I don't care what it is you do; your job knows they can always find someone else that can do what you do, but can they find someone who knows what you know? Ever wonder why companies always downsize the labor force first but never layoff the Sales or IT Department? It is a lot more difficult to replace knowledge than it is to replace laborers. If you want more long-term success, job security, and you want to invest in your future, always strive to get paid for what you know and not for what you do.

SET A STANDARD OF EXCELLENCE IN ALL YOU DO

Undoubtedly at some time we have all found ourselves uttering the words "That's so ghetto" about something or someone we felt fell short of our expectations of excellence. Perhaps some company's young receptionist was unprofessional with you or maybe during opening prayer the deaconess at your church asked the Lord to forgive the First Lady for wearing that same black hat every Sunday. Whatever your experience may have been, we have all been there at one time or another asking, "What in the world were they thinking?" We laugh at the folly of others and chalk it up as ghetto; however, your value has been seriously compromised if you are the one being called ghetto.

12 ESSENTIAL ELEMENTS FOR YOUR GREATEST COMEBACK EVER!

If you want to attract more people and build a reputable personal brand then you must live by a higher standard. You must set a standard of excellence in all you do. If you want to compete with, and hopefully one day become, the best then you have to act, think, look and operate like the best today. You may not have written the most books but you can certainly make sure that your books are excellently produced. You may not have the biggest sales department but you can strive to make sure your salespeople provide excellent service to your clients. Excellence cannot be measured quantitatively by how much you have, but it is measured qualitatively by how well you use what you have.

When you set a standard of excellence in your organization, it lets those working with you know that you only expect and accept the best. It also sends a sign to those whom you serve that you will only give them your best. Whether it is giving 100% effort on every project, starting every meeting on time or wearing a suit to work on dress down day; every detail plays a significant role in how you and your leadership are viewed by others. When you pursue excellence, those around you will also begin to pursue that same high mark. The more excellent you become the more excellent your results will be.

When people understand that you expect excellence from them it will prevent them from coming to you with just any kind of mess. They will begin to try to solve the simple problems themselves instead of bombarding you with problems they should be able to fix on their own. The more they grow the bigger the problems they will tackle. They will take pride in their performance and begin to imitate your excellent behaviors. If you want to be seen as the Most Valuable Person in your circles then start by setting a standard of excellence that promotes independent thinking and problem solving and makes everyone around you excellent too.

CREATE A BETTER YOU!
MAKE THE LIVES OF OTHERS BETTER AND THEY WILL MAKE YOUR LIFE BETTER

In his Inaugural Address of 1961, President John F. Kennedy said "Ask not what your country can do for you; ask what you can do for your country." Probably one of the most memorable Presidential Quotes of all time and that sentiment rings true when discussing how you can create better value as well. The sooner you can shift from a mindset of "What's in it for me?" to a mindset of "How many people can I help today?" the sooner you will see things open up for your life like never before. Creating a better life for yourself is directly affected by how much better you make the lives of those around you.

If people know you have their best interest in mind, and most people are motivated by their own best interests, then once they see you are there to help improve their lives, they will see it's in their best interest to keep you around. They will do all they can to make sure you stick around and continue contributing to their lives in a positive way. It sounds like a game but it's really all about knowing what motivates people and tapping into those triggers in order to garner the desired responses and outcomes.

I've seen selfish people get around a group of people who very well could have made a huge positive impact on their lives and business and yet they squandered the opportunity because of their own arrogance and self-centered goals. They go in with their sales pitch to total strangers before ever even building any type of rapport with them. Sometimes even coming off as offensive simply because they never took the time to show they cared about the potential client they were "wooing". One thing I know for sure is people hate being sold to and people hate being sold to by strangers even more. You are not going to convince anyone of your value to them when you continually show them that the most valuable person to you is yourself.

12 ESSENTIAL ELEMENTS FOR YOUR GREATEST COMEBACK EVER!

So the choice is yours. You can either go out and "Do you" and wave at all your "haters" while you make things happen by any means necessary leaving all types of human wreckage in your path along the way; or you can commit to a life of making the lives of others better and having them in turn commit to making your life better. It's really easy math when you break it down. Would you rather count on 100% of your own efforts ever day or count on 1% of the efforts of 100 people? You've struggled long enough. Make your life easier simply by making the lives of others easier by the value you bring to their lives. You deserve it.

CREATE A BETTER YOU!
Journal

Chapter Notes:

_____

_____

_____

_____

_____

_____

_____

_____

I Need To Create Better Value By:

_____

_____

_____

_____

_____

12 ESSENTIAL ELEMENTS FOR YOUR GREATEST COMEBACK EVER!

_____

_____

_____

Action Steps:

_____

_____

_____

_____

_____

_____

_____

_____

_____

CREATE A BETTER YOU!

Chapter Twelve

Create A Better

STORY

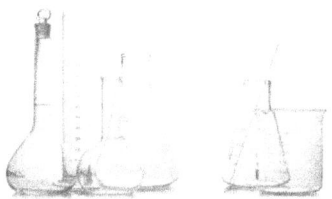

I have a confession to make. I know this is Man Law Violation to even admit this but one of my favorite songs is "I Was Here" by... BEYONCE'! There I said it! Yes I like Beyonce'. I'm by no means one of those crazed Super Fans passing out at concerts or making "Single Ladies" YouTube videos but she's made quite a few inspirational songs that have really resonated with me. That's what I love about music. There's always a song out there to speak to your mood or situation. I know I'm not the only one out there who has "Theme Songs" I hear to inspire me.

When I think about my legacy and the impact on the world I hope to leave when I'm gone, Beyonce's song just speaks to that desire in such a powerful way. This song speaks to the story I hope to leave behind. I simply want people to know I was here and my actions

12 ESSENTIAL ELEMENTS FOR YOUR GREATEST COMEBACK EVER!

positively impacted the lives of other people along the way. Check out the lyrics then go listen to the song with the music. I promise you'll be moved as well.

"I Was Here"
© Diane Warren

I wanna leave my footprints on the sands of time
Know there was something that, meant something that I left behind
When I leave this world, I'll leave no regrets
Leave something to remember, so they won't forget

I was here
I lived, I loved
I was here
I did, I've done everything that I wanted
And it was more than I thought it would be
I will leave my mark so everyone will know
I was here

I want to say I lived each day, until I died
And know that I meant something in, somebody's life
The hearts I have touched, will be the proof that I leave
That I made a difference, and this world will see

I was here
I lived, I loved
I was here
I did, I've done everything that I wanted
And it was more than I thought it would be
I will leave my mark so everyone will know

I just want them to know
That I gave my all, did my best
Brought someone some happiness
Left this world a little better just because

I was here

CREATE A BETTER YOU!

I lived, I loved
I was here
I did, I've done everything that I wanted
And it was more than I thought it would be
I wanna leave my mark so everyone will know
I was here

So what will be your story? What will be the legacy you leave behind? You can't wait until you're gone to build a story. You build it every day of your LIFE- while you're living. If you were to die today, would anyone remember your contributions 10 years from now? Would they remember in 20 years? 50 years? 100 years? What about 1,000 years?

Some people are content with living a life in which they are the only focus. But for those who want to live their best life; legacy is also important. It's not important for bragging rights, monuments or the ability to say "Hey look at me!", but it's important in the sense that it's one of the best indicators of how selfLESS a life you lived. The more people who are positively impacted by your living, the more successful your life has been when it comes to leaving a legacy and living a life of purpose.

I said earlier in this book that people are your most valuable resource. The greatest residue that you can leave behind is that of making other people's lives better because you were here. Pouring into other people as much as you can and giving them all the more reason to feel good about the impact you had on their lives is the best way to go about **CREATING A BETTER STORY**.

WHAT'S GOING TO BE YOUR LEGACY?

How are you going to live your dash? You know that little line on your tombstone between your date of birth and date of death? Your dash. How are you going to live it? What are you going to do with the rest of your life to make your dash worth it? Folks don't like talking about death but we all have to go at some point. So what if God called you home today? What kind of legacy would you have left behind up until this point? Are you cool with that? Would those whom you leave behind be cool with that? Is that really the best you could do?

The best thing about being alive is that as long as you're living, you can start over every single day. Every day is a new beginning towards creating the life you were purposed to live and cementing a legacy you and your family can be proud of. As long as you focus daily on creating a better you, then your positive legacy will grow in lockstep with your efforts. You cannot force people to regard you in the way *you* would like them to regard you so don't get caught up focusing on how every action is going to affect your legacy. You can't write that part of the story yourself. You just remain focused on doing the right things and helping the most people and when you are gone, they will write the story for you.

We are living in a world today affected by the actions of others decades, even centuries ago. We are the personification of their legacies. The world we see today is a product of the actions they made years ago and our lives are better or worse for it. What are people going to say about you 50 years from now? Just like we're standing on the shoulders of those who sacrificed for us 50 years ago, there will be people 50 years from now standing on the shoulders of your work and contributions to society. The decisions you make today will determine whether or not they're standing with smile or a frown.

Take charge of your legacy right now by simply deciding to make your life about more than just you. Decide today that you will be the one in your family tree that everyone else is thanking for changing the family's fortune and destiny. Make a choice that you will be the one to break the generational curse of financial lack in your family. Why can't you be the first one to graduate college and create a legacy of greater educational expectations in your family? It doesn't take much to

CREATE A BETTER YOU!

change the course of your life and thereby change your legacy. It does however require sacrifice and commitment. It's up to you to decide if it's worth it. Are you going to strive to make an unforgettable mark in the world while you're hear or just pass away like you never existed?

MAKE SURE PEOPLE KNOW YOU WERE HERE

Some people are destined to be the Lead Singers while others fit best in the role of Backup Singers. Some people relish the role of being the team's leading scorer while some are content being the 12th man on the end of the bench. If you have read all the way through this book then I guess it's safe to assume you want to be a lead singer. You want to make a bigger impact in the world and make sure everyone knows you were here. My question for you then is what are you going to leave behind?

When your work here is done, what are you going to leave behind to make sure people know you were here? We all leave something. What we leave is the true indicator of the legacy we've left and the story others will tell about us. The overwhelming majority of people spend their lives declaring their love to their family and friends and when they die they leave the people they love nothing but bills and debt. Nothing says "I Love You" like bill collectors calling your family after your death to collect debts your family didn't even incur. How about trying something different and leaving the world something else to remind them you were here?

How about leaving some Works? What tangible evidence of your existence will you leave behind? How many books are going to die with you that you should be writing right now instead? How many of your songs will people be singing long after you've departed this life? How many homes will you build? What kind of clothes will you design? How many movies will you direct? There has to be something in you that you could be doing right now instead of continuing to push it off. Get to work on whatever it is you were designed to create and make it happen before it's too late.

Maybe you have ideas you plan to leave behind? I know I've invented at least 4 products in my head that I never did anything with. What about you? Maybe your idea is also an invention. Or maybe you have come up with a more efficient way to achieve some task. Wouldn't it be great to have a process or law named after you? Start putting those ideas on paper and begin working out a plan to put them into action. They won't do you any good in the grave with you so you might as well share your great ideas with the world and make your mark!

Here's a new idea. How about leaving some money? Yes, leave some cash for others. Billionaires like Bill Gates and Warren Buffet have gotten so rich over their lifetimes that their new goal is to give as much money away as they can. You may never reach billionaire status but you have your entire life to work on creating income generating assets that will continue to either pay your family or whomever you decide to donate your wealth to once you go. It doesn't take millions to start a scholarship fund at your college alma mater in your name. The one thing about money I've learned over time is the more willing you are to give it away, the more room you will make to receive even more. Even if you have nothing more than a life insurance policy, that is much better than leaving the bill for the funeral behind.

Lastly, what about leaving people? A true success story of legacy isn't about how good you were, it's about how good you were at duplicating your success in the lives of others. True legacy is all about the crew of leaders you develop along the way. When you leave who is left to carry the torch? That's the essence of legacy. When you have built people up to be even better than you and continue your work once you're gone, that creates a living legacy for years to come. Build up others and you can live forever.

CREATE A BETTER YOU!
WRITE HISTORY ONE SUCCESS AT A TIME

How do you eat an elephant? One bite at a time. How do you make history? One success at a time. It's easy to get caught up in the big picture, the final destination, when you are trying to do a major work. You must be sure to not overlook the small victories along the way which lead to that final destination. If you continue to judge your success by the final picture than you will find yourself easily becoming frustrated and ready to quit when your reality doesn't quite match what you dream in your head.

I know this because it's even happened to me. I've written five books now. That's a major accomplishment! Most people will never write one and here I am penning my fifth. However, writing books was always the first phase of my big plan. Being an author was never the goal for the rest of my life. There's been many times when I've grown frustrated because eight years in, I'm still writing books. My goal was to be on to the next phase of my media company long ago. My plan had me making music, producing TV shows and directing movies by now but God's plan was different. I've had friends and loved ones slap me back to reality to appreciate all that I've accomplished even if it isn't all I hoped to do by this point.

When I looked at what God has blessed me to do up to this point, it was truly humbling. I am grateful for all I've been used to do and more importantly all the lives I've touched along the way. Even in the midst of writing this book, I received an email from a parent of a student I mentored two years ago. She thanked me for the lessons I taught in my first book and how it impacted her son who's now in college studying Video Game Design. I had to really shake my head at myself at the idea of what would have happened to that kid had I quit on my purpose because I was frustrated that I wasn't reaching my goals fast enough?

12 ESSENTIAL ELEMENTS FOR YOUR GREATEST COMEBACK EVER!

I once heard John C. Maxwell say "Success doesn't happen in a day, it happens daily". Every day we have to choose to pursue success and appreciate the progress we make each day. Some days are for us and some days are for those watching us. Never give up and never surrender along the way. Enough little victories eventually add up to a huge victory. Celebrate every win along the way and know it's one more stone on your path to success. When it's all said and done, people will be celebrating the greatness of your life all because you decided to create a better YOU!

CREATE A BETTER YOU!
Journal

Chapter Notes:

_____
_____
_____
_____
_____
_____
_____
_____

I Need To Create A Better Story By:

_____
_____
_____
_____
_____

12 ESSENTIAL ELEMENTS FOR YOUR GREATEST COMEBACK EVER!

_____

_____

_____

Action Steps:

_____

_____

_____

_____

_____

_____

_____

_____

CREATE A BETTER YOU!

Conclusion

Create A Better

YOU!

So there you have it. I've given you the twelve elements to creating a better life by creating a better YOU. Easy lessons that you can begin right away in order to start living the life you were designed to live. So what are you going to do now? Are you going to put this book up on the shelf with the rest of them or are you going to really implement the training given and change your life today? You no longer can use not knowing as your excuse for not creating a better life for yourself.

I didn't just write this book, I lived it. So I know it works and more importantly I know whatever excuses you come up with as to why this won't work for you are bologna. It's time to start taking responsibility for your life and your actions. It's time for you to become the best YOU possible and you are holding in your hands the blueprint to achieving that. But this book is just Step #1. I have developed an entire system to help Create A Better YOU!

I'm not just going to write this book and send you on your way telling you "Good luck with that." I have put in place a system of

12 ESSENTIAL ELEMENTS FOR YOUR GREATEST COMEBACK EVER!

resources to assist and coach you along your journey. All you have to do is visit www.RyanCGreene.com to see how you can partake in all of the resources to help you succeed. When you're ready to take it to the next level, you can register for a live "Create A Better YOU!" Webinar. For those who are serious about experience their greatest comeback, the Create A Better YOU! Digital University is even available.

Nothing excites me more than hearing the success stories from those who have read my books. I write these books to help people just like you. I know if I had someone mentoring me earlier in life then I would have reached my goals much sooner. I love being that mentor for others. I believe in giving you the truth above all else. Sometimes that truth comes out sweet and makes you feel good; sometimes it comes out like a Mike Tyson Punch and knocks you down. No matter how it feels, know my words come from a place of love and genuine desire to help you **CREATE A BETTER YOU!**

CREATE A BETTER YOU!

ABOUT THE AUTHOR

SPEAKER - AUTHOR - ENTREPRENEUR

Ryan C. Greene graduated from Hampton University in Hampton, VA with a Bachelors of Science Degree in Marketing. He currently resides in Mitchellville, MD and is quickly becoming one of the most sought after speakers and trainers on the East Coast. In January 2005, Ryan founded Bakari Book Publishers (now GreeneHouse Media) and published his first book, *"Success Is In Your Hand: 19 Keys To Unlocking The Successful Person You Were Designed To Be"*. His second book, *"My Little Black Book Of Leadership: 15 Leadership Lessons I Learned From My Ex-Girlfriends"*, was released in the March 2008. In December 2008 Ryan released his third book, *"Lead Wolf vs. Lone Wolf: You're Only A Leader If Others Are Following"* followed by his fourth book, the Amazon.com #1 Best Seller, *"The Queens' Legacy"* in April 2009. Ryan's fifth book *"Create A Better YOU!"* was released January 2013.

In January 2006, Ryan became the Executive Producer and Host of his own weekly radio talk show, **"The Ryan C Greene Show"**. In November 2010, Ryan began co-hosting a weekly radio show, **"The Ryan and Bryan Show"** with Bryan Johnson. Through his media company, Ryan hopes to change as many lives as possible by delivering high-impact relevant solutions for unlocking one's full potential and realizing their individual destiny and purpose. Ryan is also jumping into film and television production and most recently began hosting and executive producing two Web TV shows **"Create A Better YOU!"** and **"Sell More Books Now!"** and is developing two family game shows.

12 ESSENTIAL ELEMENTS FOR YOUR GREATEST COMEBACK EVER!

Ryan speaks from the heart and his genuine, thought-provoking, and humorous presentations have already changed countless lives. He has been featured in a wide array of print, radio and television media. He has been a contributing writer for several magazines as well as guest hosted several radio and television talk shows. Ryan has served on the Advisory Board of Morgan State University's Entrepreneurial Development Assistance Center, was the Membership Coordinator for the Association of Black Media Workers, the Baltimore Chapter of the National Black Journalists Association and currently sits on the Board Of Directors for a non-profit, Gifts Of Precious Stone. Ryan is also the Founder & Executive Director of The Jacqueline M Kidd Foundation, a non-profit foundation named after his mother that donates money for sickle-cell research and awards college scholarships to youth with the disease.

For more information or to book Ryan C. Greene to speak for your organization or to present at your next event, please visit www.RyanCGreene.com or email Ryan@RyanCGreene.com

Check Out These Other Best Selling Titles By Ryan C. Greene
www.RyanCGreene.com

Success Is In Your Hand

My Little Black Book Of Leadership

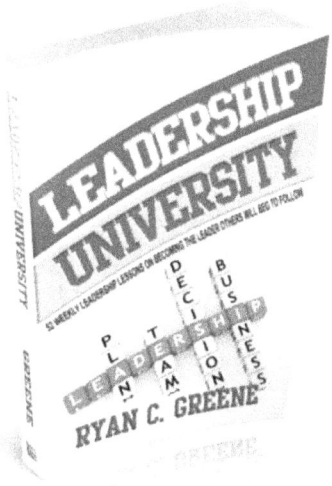

Leadership University

Experience "THE PASSIONPRENEUR" At Your Next Event

Ryan C. Greene
www.RyanCGreene.com

Keynote Speaker | Workshop Leader | Best Selling Author | Media Personality

Ryan C. Greene has been influencing audiences since 2004, with his transformational messages of maximizing the total You. He is the preeminent speaker on Leadership Development, Walking In Your Purpose, and Living A Passion-Driven Life. Book Ryan to speak at your next conference, team training, staff development workshop, retreat, or special event.

RE-IGNITE YOUR FIRE WITHIN
Let your PASSION be your life's compass. In this presentation Ryan C. Greene empowers you to reclaim your purpose, rekindle your passion, and revive your dreams, so that you can begin living your most passionate and profitable life every day!

CREATE A BETTER YOU!
If you want a better life, you must create a better YOU! Discover the "12 Elements To Creating A Better YOU" in this powerful presentation about overcoming setbacks and bouncing back. Get ready for your greatest comeback ever!

15 LEADERSHIP LESSONS I LEARNED FROM MY EX-GIRLFRIENDS
Leadership is all about relationships. In this one-of-a-kind training Ryan takes you on a journey like no other leadership training ever has! Hear entertaining stories of past relationships and learn how they can make you a top-notch leader.

UNLOCK THE SUCCESSFUL PERSON YOU WERE DESIGNED TO BE
Ryan gives you a roadmap for reaching your full potential, fulfilling your purpose, and becoming the successful person you were designed to be.

AFTER YOU SAY, "I DON'T"
Overcoming divorce, depression, and delayed purpose. After losing everything and suffering through a failed marriage, Ryan gives insight, advice, and encouragement on how to overcome the pain of divorce, bounce back from depression, and reclaim your delayed purpose.

RAVE REVIEWS FOR THE
PASSIONPRENEUR

"I am a firm believer that learning, growing, and transforming should be enjoyable and fun. Ryan definitely makes the process of learning leadership an engaging journey."
~ Delatorro L. McNeal, II, MSP, Peak Performance Expert, Platinum Performance Global

"Ryan was very professional and a joy to work with. His customized presentation was just what our group needed!"
~ Diane Timmons-Himes, State Independent Living Coordinator, MD Dept. of Human Resources

"Ryan's leadership training at our annual Leadership Conference was the most requested program by the attendees so we HAD to bring him back again!"
~ Opel T. Jones, Director, Hampton University William R. Harvey Leadership Institute

Book Ryan Today And Get Ready To Unleash Your
PURPOSE • POWER • PASSION

Ryan has written the book on Success and Leadership

National Talk Show Host

You've been searching for a dynamic keynote speaker, engaging workshop leader and powerful motivator. You seek a presenter who delivers results driven, ground-breaking presentations. A speaker who teaches innovative content in an interactive and entertaining way. Now you've found him! Best Selling Author & Professional Speaker, Ryan C. Greene will bring your organization to life as he propels your group to higher heights, greater productivity, and a renewed sense of purpose and direction. Be your organization's Rock Star by booking Ryan C. Greene today! *(Partial Client List)*

Connect With Ryan:
- /IAmRyGPage
- @IAmRyG
- /IAmRyG
- /c/RyanCGreene

GREENE HOUSE MEDIA

Ryan C. Greene is ready to help your organization reach higher heights! Contact Ryan and book today!

www.RyanCGreene.com

@ Ryan@RyanCGreene.com ☎ 443.380.0995

P.O. Box 2222 | Bowie, MD 20718

#100AUTHORCHALLENGE
DO YOU HAVE THE WRITE STUFF?

GreeneHouse Media is signing 100 NEW AUTHORS!

All Published & Unsigned Authors
Are You Ready To Tell Your Story?
Join The #100AuthorChallenge

GreeneHouse Media is looking for **100 new all-star writers** who are ready to **CRUSH IT** as best selling authors! If you have a strong story to tell, GreeneHouse Media wants you on our winning team. Are you ready to accept the #100AuthorChallenge?

www.100AuthorChallenge.com

New Show Every Week

Available on iTunes

tunein

The Passionpreneurs Podcast
Hosted by Ryan C. Greene

www.ThePassionpreneurs.com

www.ingramcontent.com/pod-product-compliance
Lightning Source LLC
Chambersburg PA
CBHW050556300426
44112CB00013B/1939